THE RAPTURE
of the
CHURCH
BEFORE AND AFTER

JEANIE BREEDWELL

Copyright © 2020 by Jeanie Breedwell.

ISBN   Softcover   978-1-951469-64-1

All rights reserved. No part of this book may be reproduced or transmitted in any form or by any means, electronic or mechanical, including photocopying, recording, or by any information storage and retrieval system without express written permission from the author, except in the case of brief quotations embodied in critical reviews and certain other non-commercial uses permitted by copyright law.

Printed in the United States of America.

To order additional copies of this book, contact:
Bookwhip
1-855-339-3589
https://www.bookwhip.com

BOOK 1

FOREWORD

The moral of my story… Lots of people are not worried about their souls. They go on with their lives like nothing is going to happen. Our world is in a chaos, upside down. Jesus is coming soon. It is time to get ready. Judgment day is ahead for them that are not looking for our Lord. It says in God's word you can be saved if you believe Jesus died for us so we can go to heaven, if we confess our sins.

JESUS IS COMING. ARE YOU READY?

It was a very pretty day in Georgia. It was the fall of the year. The trees were so pretty and brown. Some flowers began to bloom. Now this was almost impossible, because flowers bloom in spring. But the Bible is coming true every day, so you cannot tell the weather what is going to happen.

In this title town in Georgia where was getting different, it would say on the news the weather was going to be sunny, then it would rain. And the wind would get high, blowing real hard… The town of Jordan was looking for Jesus.

As the day unfolded, people in the town began to look at the sky. There was something in the air that made everyone wondered what it was that day. They knew the rapture was close. It was heard in stories.

Mary went to Walgreens with her friend. There she heard in the next aisle two women talking." You know, it feels like something going to happen," said one of the women. "I have been reading my Bible, and I know that Jesus is coming real soon."

"Yes," said the other lady. "I know the preacher has been telling everyone to get ready. It is real close."

Mary hurried over to get into the conversation. "My name is Mary. I live just over the hill. I heard what you all were talking about, and my mother and dad read to my brother and me the Bible and we have been talking about Jesus's coming. We believe it is soon."

"How old are you little girl?"

"I am nine years old."

"Well, that should tell us something. Because the Bible says out of little child comes the truth."

"Yes, you are right. Well, little girl, I have got to go."

"Me too," said the other lady.

"My name is Mary."

"Yes. What did you say?" asked one of the women.

"Oh, my name is Mary. You know like in the Bible, Jesus's mother, her name was Mary."

"Sure," said the lady.

Mary began to get what she came for so she could find her friend, Terry. When she started to pay, the lady looked at her strangely.

"Are you okay, honey?"

"Yes, why?" said Mary.

"Well, you look so white like you may have seen a ghost."

"Well," said Mary, "we were talking about Jesus coming back. Two ladies I ran into on the store."

"What two ladies? I have been here all day, and there was one person that paid for their things before you."

"No," said Mary, "they were talking to me about Jesus."

"Well, I do not know what you are talking about."

So Mary finished her conversation by telling the lady Jesus is coming back. "Are you ready?"

"Oh, that is what you were taking about."

"Yes, don't you believe it?"

"Well, maybe. But this has been talked about for many years, and nothing happened."

So Mary walked out the door. Her friend was waiting for her, but she did not say anything about what happened. She was in shock. She said to herself, "I will talk to Mom about it."

"Mary, do you want to go to my house now?"

"No, Terry, I want to go home. If Jesus comes tonight I want to be with my family, so we can go together."

"Do really believe that, about Jesus?"

"Yes he is coming. Terry, are you ready?"

"What do you mean?"

"Well you have got to be born again."

"I cannot do that. My mom cannot have me the second time."

"No, that is not what I am talking about. You sound like Nicodemus in the Bible.

"Well, I do not read the Bible, and my mom does not read it to me."

"Terry, would you like to know Jesus?"

"I do not know; maybe later."

"Terry, today is the day of the Lord. He may come tonight."

"Well, I will later."

"Okay, Terry, I tried." A tear dropped from Mary's eyes, as she got out of the car. She reached to hug her friend. She said a prayer.

When Mary entered her house, her mother was going upstairs. "Mother."

"Yes."

"I have to talk to you."

"Okay, can it wait for one minute while I put the clothes away?"

"Sure, Mother," Mary said, as she followed her mom upstairs.

"Mom, do you think Jesus will come tonight?"

"He could why?"

"Well, because I was talking to my friend, Terry, and she does not know about Jesus."

"What are you saying?"

"Well on the way here, I asked her if she was saved, and she did not know what I was talking about. Mom, she is putting in off. I do not think she believe he is coming."

"Well, honey, you need tell her about the Bible. Tell her Jesus died for her, and he loves her so much. Maybe she will change."

"I sure hope so," said Mary. "I have been friend for a while to her."

"I know don't they go to church."

"Yes, Mom, I think so."

"Is that what you wanted to talk to me about?"

"Some of it."

"What is the rest?"

"Today, I went to the store with Terry and her mom. While I was there, I heard two ladies talking about Jesus's coming, so got I into their conversation, and we talked a while."

"Well, what happened?

"Well, they left, and I got what I went for. When I got though, I went to pay for my things, and the lady made a remark that I look white ion the face. I began to tell her about the ladies, and she said no one had checked out there, except one man. Mom, was it angels I saw?"

"Maybe they walked out the door."

"No, Mom, I saw them go up there."

"Well, honey, you could have come in contract with angels."

"Mom, are you going to read the Bible tonight?"

"Yes, Mary, what do you want me to read about?"

"What about Jesus's coming?"

"Okay, that is in Matt."

"Mom, things are changing."

"Yes, honey, they are. Where is your brother?"

"He is playing ball in the yard."

"Mary, you need to do your room."

"Okay, Mom."

"I will I put some clean sheets on your bed, you can make it up."

"Okay, Mom, I will."

"And can you make your brother's bed too?"

"Okay, I will? What is supper tonight?"

"Well, it is your dad's dish. He likes it so much, that is baked chicken."

"Yes, I like it too," said Mary.

"And greens too and bake beans. We can top it off with pie."

"Good, Mom."

"Blackberry, I know everyone likes that with ice cream."

"Yes, Mom."

"Now you get your room clean and your brother's."

"I will, Mom. When is dad is coming home?"

"Soon, I think. He did call to say he would be a little late."

Mary went to Steve's room; he was not there.

"Mom-"

"Yes."

"Steve is still playing in the yard. He is not in his room."

"Tell him to come in."

"Okay, Mom, I will.

"Steve, where are at? said Mary. She began to look for him, and she kept calling him.

She saw him at a friend's house across the street.

"Steve, Mom wants you."

"What for?" said Steve.

"She said dad would be home soon, and we will be eating."

"Okay, I am coming. Roy, I will see you later."

"What we were talking about, do you believe that?" said Roy.

"Yes, I do," said Steve. "My mother read the Bible to us. We have a family get-together every night. Would you like to come over our house tonight and eat with us? Afterward Mom will read the Bible."

"Sure, I will need to call my mom. She is at work."

"That is okay," said Steve.

"Okay, hold on while I call."

"We will be waiting for you," said Steve.

In a little while, Roy came out the door. "Mom said it will be okay."

"Good," replied Steve.

"But I need to get home before dark."

"I will walk you home," said Steve.

As they were crossing the street, Roy wanted to talk about the Bible. "Steve my mom does not want me to talk about God."

"Why? Steve asked in return."

"She and my dad do not believe in God." I go to my grandmother sometimes, and she takes me to church and tells me Jesus is coming back. She believes in the rapture. They all that go to that church talk about the rapture, but when I go home everything is not the same."

"Well, I hope that we can help you."

As they entered the door, Steve said, "Mom, this is my friend, Roy."

"Never mind, where have you all been? Your dad is on way home. Sorry, what is your name?"

"My name is Roy. I am sorry too. It was my mistake. I had to call Mom after your son asked me to come over to listen to you read the Bible.

"Okay, that is good," said Mrs. Smith.

"Come and go with me to my room," said Steve, "I will show you my new computer that mom and dad got me Christmas."

"Okay."

The Rapture of the Church

"Mom let me know when Dad gets home, okay?"

"Yes, I will. Mary, go into my room and bring my Bible to me. Your dad wants me to read John 3: 16, and I will read more whatever God puts on my heart."

"Mom, here it is," said Mary.

"Thanks," replied Mary's mother.

"I hear Dad come up."

"Good, I was setting the table. Steve, come on, bring your little friend."

"I am coming. Roy, do you drink tea?"

"Yes, thank you."

"Okay, you will sit at the end of the table."

"Okay, you will sit at the end of the table."

"Hi, honey, how did it go to work?"

"Okay, I guess."

"How was your day? Mine was okay too."

"Who do we have here?" said Mr. Smith.

"Dad, this is my friend, Roy. He lives in the brown house across the street.

"Glad to have you Roy. Did Steve tell you about our family getting everyone in the living room to listen to Mrs. Smith read the Bible?

"Yes, I did."

"So want to say and be part of our family?"

"Yes, I do."

"Okay, we will start after supper."

"Good, said Roy."

"How are you mom and dad?" said Mr. Smith.

"Okay, I guess. I do not stay around them too much."

"Why is that?" Mr. Smith asked reply.

"Well, they are not too nice to one another like you all."

"Sorry, I hope things will be better for your family in the future."

"Me too," said Roy.

"Who is ready for a piece of blackberry pie and ice cream?"

"I am," said Steve.

"Me too," replied Mary.

"What about you, Roy, would you like a piece of pie?"

"Okay, thank you."

"Roy, do you have any sister and brothers?"

"No, I am the only child."

"Well, said Mr. Smith, "I bet you are lonely."

"Sometimes I am."

"Everyone that is through, retire into the living room. I will be there soon. I need to clean off the table."

"Can I help you with the dishes?" Roy asked.

"No, I can do it. Do you wash you dishes at your house?"

"Yes, I do. Mom does not have anyone to help her, so I do."

"That is so nice of you."

"I do not mind. Mom is not too well, so I try to help out as much as I can."

"How old are you, Roy?"

"I will be eleven. My next birthday is next month."

"You are real young."

"Yes, I am."

Steve is twelve years old. He will have his birthday in July.

"Well, everyone I am going to read from John 3: 16,' for God so love the world he gave his only son who so every believe in him should not perish have every lasting life.'"

"What does that mean?" Roy asked.

"Roy, do you know how to be saved?"

"No."

"Well, would you like to?"

"I guess."

"Okay, let me lead you in a word of prayer," said Mrs. Smith.

"Let me do it, Mom."

"Okay, son."

"Roy, my friend, Jesus loves you so much he went to the cross to give his life for you.

"Do you believe that?" said Steve.

"Yes, I do."

"Okay, then repeat after me. 'Dear Jesus, I come to you a sinner. I know you died for me, and I ask you to forgive me of my sins. I promise to live for you and honor you commands in the sweet name of Jesus, amen.' Now, Roy, you belong to Jesus."

"I do," he replied.

"Yes, son, you do," said Mrs. Smith, "as they all welcome him in.

"Mom, Roy has got to home. I told him I would walk with him so he won't be alone."

"Okay, son, your dad can go with you. Tom, you need do walk with the boys. Roy has got to go home."

"Okay, Dad," said Steve.

"We will be right back."

"Okay, Tom."

"Mom, I feel so strange for what happened at the store," said Mary.

"Well, it seems as though you may have saw two angels."

"You think so, Mom?"

"Yes, I do. Its getting close to the coming for our Lord, and things began to happen."

"Mom, can I call Grandma. I feel she is so lonely without Grandpa. He has been gone so long, and when I see Grandma, she seems so sad."

"Honey, she is okay, She is so old, and she loves God so much and she wanted to go home. She told me she knows it will not be long."

"Mom, tell me about Jesus."

"Well, honey, I do tell you when I read God's word, how he came here as a baby. Mary was told by an angel she was going to have Jesus."

"Mary was married, was she mother?"

"yes honey, she was ; but Joseph was her friend. They went together, and they were seen at lots of places at the time Mary was having Jesus."

"Mother, Jesus was born in a manager?"

"Yes, Mary, he was. There was no room at the inn. Mary we will finished this later, you need to turn the light on for you brother dad."

"Okay, Mom I will. Mom, I see Dad and Steve coming back."

"Good. It is getting late, and we have got to go bed. Windy, do you know what Roy told us?"

"Yes, Mom, he is scared to tell his mom and dad he got saved."

"Why?" Mrs. Smith asked.

"I will go by their house tomorrow and talk to his family, see what they say," said her husband. "Yes, I will break the ice."

"Well, it is getting late time for us all to say good night. Good night, Mom; good night, Dad," said Mary.

"Don't forget to pray."

"I won't, Mom. I want to pray for Rev; he needs someone to pray for him."

"That is good, Mary. I will also pray for him and his family."

Mary went to her room. "Well, I will pray now," She began to pray. "Father, first of all, I want to thank you for letting Roy come into our life so we could lead him to you. I do not know his mom and dad, but you do. Now I ask in your name to let Roy lead his family to you, and I thank you, Father, with all my love, your small daughter and friend forever, amen."

The next day was Saturday. Mary heard mother in the kitchen as she passed the door.

"Mother, what are you cooking? Smell's real good."

"Well, you know how much your dad likes hams and eggs."

"Yes, Mom, he also likes your biscuits with plenty of butter."

"Yes, honey, he does."

"Mother, I need to ask you something."

"What, Mary?"

"Remember Roy said his birthday is next month?"

"Yes, he did, why?"

"Because I thought it would be nice to give him a birthday party at our house."

"Yes sure, we can do that. You talk to your brother and see if he can find out what Roy would like for his birthday. Tell him not to spill the surprise."

"Okay, Mom, I will do that. Are you going to their house today? And talk to his mom and dad about him getting saved."

"Yes, I think so, but you go now and call dad and brother to breakfast."

"Dad, Steve, come to eat," said Mary. She had not go the words out of her mouth when her dad appeared.

"What is that smell, so good, Windy?"

"Something you like."

"Yes," Dad said, "Mary dig in."

"Where is Steven at?" asked his mom.

"I will go get him," said Mary.

"Okay, honey."

You could hear Mary down the hallway, calling her brother, Steve.

"Yes, Mary."

"Time to eat."

"Okay, I will be there in a little."

"Hurry, Mom is waiting on you."

"You better get here," said Mary.

"Here I am," said Steve.

"Do want milk to drink," said his mom.

"Yes, that is fine."

"Mom, let's talk about the birthday party."

"What birthday?" said Steve.

"We were talking about having Roy a party on his birthday, and I need you to find out what he would like," said his mom.

"Okay, I think I know.

"What are you talking about?" asked his mom.

"Well, Mom, they are very poor people, and his mom does not make much money and his dad is not working."

"Why?" said Mr. Smith.

"Because he is not working, he has to look for work but can't find any."

"Okay, maybe we can help them some."

"Would you, Mom?" said Steve.

"Sure, won't we, Tom?"

"Sure we can."

"Mom, may I go over to Roy? I will find out what he would like for his birthday."

"No, not now, son. I want to go over and talk to his parents, but I have got to do the dishes."

"Mom, I will help you with the dishes, if you want me to."

"Mary, you can clean your room. I will do the dishes and get some clothes in the washing before I go. No hurry. I have got all day, they may go somewhere."

"But, Mom, you said I could go over there."

"I know, I will go over in a little. I won't be gone too long."

So Mrs. Smith got ready. "Mary, I am going over to see Roy's mom and dad. If they are home, I will be back soon."

"Okay, Mom."

"Now, Mary, do not forget to clean your room."

"That is what I am going to do now."

Mary went into her mom. She began to think about what good parents her and her brother had. She knelt down and began to pray. "Father, be with my mother when she meets Roy's family. I pray she can lead them both to you. I do not know them, but I am they are good people as their son is."

"And Lord, I am only nine years old. I guess I am smart for my age. Could you use me to tell little children about you and how much you love us? I want to live for you and do your commands, be a blessing to someone. Now, Lord, bless my family look after them and never let them go the wrong way. Also, Lord, I pray for Roy and his family, that when my mom talks to them that they will give their lives to you. Now, Lord, I have got to clean my room. Hold on, Lord, I want to remember Terry. Lord, speak to Terry's heart, amen."

As Mrs. Smith knocked on the Johnson's door, someone opened the door.

"Yes, can I help you?" A little woman was standing at the door. She had long brown hair,

very pretty. Her age was forty or maybe forty-five; she looked real retired.

"Yes, my name is Windy. I live across the street."

"I know who you are. My son was nonstop talking about you people, said you all lead him to Jesus. Now I got real mad when he told me this. But I had a dream that a dream that same night about Jesus coming. He was in the clouds. I looked up the sky, and he was on a white horse. I was scared because I know I was not right. I need to change, I said to myself. Then I woke up, got down on my knees, and I prayed to Jesus, please, Lord, help me do not let me go to hell."

"So you got saved?"

"Yes, I did. My husband, I did not tell."

"Why?"

"Because he does not understand; he was raised different than me. My mother is a born-again. She believe in God been serving him so long. She took us to church, and she believes in the rapture."

"Yes, that is what your son said. He is friends with my boy, Steve. My son led him to the Lord."

"Well, where is your husband at?"

"He is gone fishing, I think."

"Well I will be praying for your family."

"Thank you very much."

As Mrs. Smith started to leave, she took her hand. "Here, I hope his can help you all. My name is Mrs. Windy Smith, glad to meet you."

My name is Mrs. Mary Johnson, glad to meet you."

"My daughter's name is Mary."

"Is that right?"

"Yes it is. My son is Steve, and my husband is Tom. Now if you every need anything, let me know, and you all come to our home. We have our Bible reading after supper, and we have that time to our family. Anytime you all want to come over, come on, you are welcome."

"Yes, today is my day off. I am at work through the week."

As Mrs. Smith starts to leave, she hugs her new friend, and she left.

When Mrs. Smith got home, her husband and son were in living room, watching TV.

"Well I had a great day with the Johnson across the street."

"What happened?" asked her son Steve.

"God was with me today. Roy's mom got saved."

"Really?" said her husband.

"Yes, I did not have any thought of what to say. She broke conversation herself. Something happened that made her change her mind. She told me."

"Was her husband there?" asked Tom.

"No, he went fishing. We were alone. She told me she did not want him to know she got saved because he does not believe in God."

"That is bad. Windy, do you think he would listen to me?"

"You can try, but you had better pray before you go. For how Mary talks about him, he is a bad cookie."

"I will ask God to help me."

"He will," said his wife.

In came Mary, the daughter. "What are you all talking about?" said Mary. "Oh, Mom, you went over to see Roy, Steve's friend, Mom?"

"Yes, I did."

"How did it go?"

"Well, she was by herself, and we talked."

"What did she say, Mom?" asked Mary.

"Well, honey, she got saved."

"While you were there?" Mary asked again.

"No, she had something happen to her."

"And that caused her to get saved?" said Mary.

"Yes, that is what she told me," said her mother.

"That is good," said Mary, "isn't it?"

"Yes, it is," said her mother.

"Windy, I saw her husband pull in, I think I will go and talk to him," said her husband.

"Okay."

He leans over her places a kiss on her lips. "See you in a little."

"Can I go?" asked Steve.

"No, son, another time, I am going for a little, will be back soon."

"Okay, Dad, if Roy is home tell him to come over."

"Yes, I will," said Tom, as he left.

"Mother, I have got to get things ready for church," said Mary, as left the room. "Mom, I did pray for you, and Roy's family."

"Well, think you. God answered your prayer, I see he did."

Mr. Smith knocked at the Johnson's door. It opened, and in front of him stood a well-dressed man with a little long hair, big blue eyes, and he look tired.

"Yes, can I help you?"

Mr. Smith laughed. "I live across the street. Your son, Roy, is friends with my son, Steve."

"Oh yes, he told me he met anew friend. So you are the dad?"

Yes, I am."

"Well, glad to know you. Come on in. I just had a shower from going fishing."

"Is your son home? Steve wanted me to ask if he could go over the play."

"Roy."

"Yes, Dad," his son said, as he entered the room. "Hi, Mr. Smith," said Roy.

"How are you?"

"I am fine, you okay?"

"Yes, I feel real good."

"Son, do you want to go over to your friend's house? His dad said his son asked for you to go and play."

"Yes, Dad, I do."

"Okay, you be home by dark."

"I will," he said, and he left.

"The reason I came over is I just bought me a pole, and it has been some time since I have been fishing. Would you like to go? Maybe next Saturday?"

"That sounds good. I went today and caught three catfish. Where you go?"

"Well, there is a nice fishing hole three miles north of here."

"I have a boat we can take out, and I like going early. What about you?"

"That will be fine," said Mr. Smith. "Okay, it is a date. Do you want to take the boys with us?" said Mr. Smith.

"That will be great," said Mr. Johnson. By the way, what is your name?"

"My name is Tom. Well, good to meet someone to go fishing with. I really like fishing."

"Me too," said Mr. Smith, "but I am a little rusty right now."

"You stay around me, you will fish all the time."

When Roy go to the Smith's, he knocked the door. Mrs. Smith opened the door.

"Hi, Roy, what is up with you?"

"Mr. Smith told my dad Steve wanted me to come over."

"Steve, your friend, Roy, is here," said Mrs. Smith.

"I will be there in a little, Mom. Tell Roy to sit down."

"Okay, you can sit down on the chair and watch TV. Steve will be here in a little."

"Okay, Mrs. Smith."

"Roy, how are you doing at school since you got saved?"

"Okay, I guess. I do not talk that much at school. I only have a couple of friends that I play with, mainly your son. We have played together at school when the teacher lets us have a break."

"I am glad you Steve get along, and you both are saved. Do you pray at night before you go to bed?"

"Yes, I do."

"Have you told your dad you got saved?"

"No, not yet; my mom, she was okay with it."

"Yes, your mom got saved. Did she tell you?"

"No, but I am glad. I knew something had happened. Mom does act different than she did a few days ago."

"How?"

"Well, she is more nice than she was."

"I am glad that your mom got saved."

"Me too."

In walked Mr. Smith.

"Well, how did it go?" asked this wife. Are you all going fishing?
"Yes, he liked idea."
"Well, good," said his wife.
"Honey, where is Steve?"
"He will be out soon. I think he is doing his homework."
"But tomorrow is Sunday."
"Well, I guess he is catching up early."
"Steve, come here," said his dad.
"Coming."
"Would you and Roy like go fishing next Saturday?"
"Sure, Dad."
"Well, we have made plans to go, but we will be leaving early. Can you and Roy get up early?"
"Yes, I will get in bed at around nine so I can get up."
"Okay, what are we having for supper?"
"I fried some chicken and made some potato and gravy and green beans. "We are going to top it off with pie."
"Good, Roy, do you want to eat with us?"
"I would, but Dad said for me to be home before dark."
"Okay, maybe some other time."
"Mom, Roy and I are going to my room and play.
"Okay, son."
"Roy, go on. I will be in there in a little while. Okay, Mom, I am going to ask Roy what he wants for his birthday. Remember, we talked about that?"
"Yes, son, you go on play.
"Okay, Mom."
"Well, Tom, how did you like your talk with James? Is that his name?
"He had got another name, but he goes by James."
"Oh, how was his company?"
"He was, okay, I guess. He sure likes to fish. His catch were three catfish today."
"He leaves early, so that means you will be getting up early?"

"Yes, Steve and me."
"Well, Mary set the table, time to eat."
"Okay, Mom, I will."
Mary began to get the plates out and set the table.
"Honey, she is so little but she does a good job."
"Yes, I am so proud of her. She is growing so fast," said her mom, as kissed her on the face.
"Stop, Mom, your mouth has water on it."
"Well, I did drink some Coke."
"Steve you and Roy come on and eat," said Mary.
"Roy cannot stay," said her mom
"Why?"
"Because he has got to be home before dark."
"Okay."
In walks Steve.
"See you later, Steve," said Roy.
"You sure you do not want to stay and eat with us?"
"No, not this time; got to go home. It is getting dark."
"Okay, see you. Mom."
"Yes, Steve."
"I know what Roy wants for his birthday."
"What?"
"Well, he said would like a fishing pole. Really, that is what he told me. He wants to go fishing real bad."
"Well, we won't get the pole until his birthday. But you can let him borrow one of yours."
"Yes, Mom, I can."
"You do have to, and it says in God's word give one if you have to. But you can let him borrow one, because we will buy him one at his birthday. You did not give our secret away, did you?"
"No, Mom, he does not know."
"Okay, well let's finish eating, and we will have our Bible study, and since we have been talking about Mathew, we will go there. And since we are talking about giving, our study is going to be chapter 6, verse 19."

"Okay, Mom, we are ready."

Everyone retired to the living room. So that is what they did as Mrs. Smith turned her Bible to Mathew: "Lay not up for yourselves treasures upon earth where moth and rust does corrupt, and where thieves break through and steal but lay up for yourselves treasures in heaven where no one can still from you."

"Mom, is that what we supposed to do?"

"Yes, Mary."

"So you are telling me that by giving his pole to Roy, Steve will one day be in heaven."

"I guess it will be known that Steve gave his friend a pole. Also, I helped his family not because I want people to know; I just wanted to,"

"Mom, why don't you go through our things and give Roy's family some of them,"

"You are right, Mary, I can do that."

"Mom, it is only a few days till his birthday. We need to get things together," said Mary.

"Yes, you are right. I will make him a cake. And, Mary, you can go with me to the store to get candles for this cake. We will need eleven of them. And we need to talk to the kids around here, see if they want to come."

"Mom, I know some, and I can ask."

"Okay, Mary, you can do it after school Monday; that we will be a good time. Now we got off the subject of the Bible, I need to get you all to bow your heads while I say a prayer. Dear Lord, thank you for this day. And my family you have blessed us so much, we thank you for that. Now I want to say a prayer for the Johnsons. Be with them, dear Lord. Let Mr. Johnson come to you. He needs you; help his family in Jesus's name, amen.'

"Okay guys, time to go in and watch TV before bedtime."

"Mom, do you think Jesus will come tonight?"

"He could, Mary?

That is good, Mom. Dad, I hope you can help Mr. Smith to come to the Lord."

"Me too, Mary."

"I know you will be happy to go fishing. It has been so long," said Mrs. Smith.

"Yes, honey it has. I know the boys will be glad."

"Yes, Dad, I will. We can catch a lot of fish."

"Mom, I wrote down what we need for the party."

"Good, Mary."

"Okay guys, time for bed. Do not forget Sunday in church, get everything ready."

"Mom, I cannot found my shoes," said Mary.

"Look in your closet, in your shoe bag."

"Okay, Mom, I will. Good night, Mom and Dad."

"Good night, Mary." Mary hugged her parents. "See you all in the morning."

"Okay, Mary," said her mother, "do not forget to pray."

"I won't, Mom."

When Mary got into her room, she found her shoes where her mom said they would be.

"I found them, Mom."

"Okay, honey, have a good night."

"You too, Mom."

Well I have got to pray. Dear Lord, thank for my parents. They are so good to my brother and me. And Lord, be with my dad and my brother's new friends and us at church Sunday. Thank you Lord, amen.

Before Mary went to bed she dropped by her brother's room. "Steve, do not forgot to pray. Jesus could come tonight."

"Okay, Mary, I won't. See in the morning."

As Mary left his room, she went to her bed. The next morning, Mary got up. She went to the bathroom. She could hear her mother in the kitchen.

"Mary is that you?"

"Yes, Mom."

"Will you get your brother up? We have got to get ready for church."

"Yes, Mom. Steve, are you up?"

No answer, Mary knocked and called out, "Steve!"

"Yes, I am up."

"Mom said for you to get ready to eat, and we are going to church."

"Steve, I made some eggs. Do you want anything else?"

"No, Mom, that is okay."

"Mary, you have the same. Is that okay?"

"Yes, Mom."

"Okay, well, let's eat."

As they all sat down, the mother said, "Tom, you say the blessing."

"Dear Lord, we want to thank you for our food and for our family. Lord, be with us at church, bless our pastor and the ones in church, amen."

"Amen," said Mrs. Smith. "Tom, do you all have any things to do at church?"

"Not now, maybe the pastor will have something lined up next week."

"Well, it is getting close, so we need to get ready," said Mrs. Smith, as she left the room. The other left also.

"When will we be leaving?" said Mary

"Soon," said her dad, "get ready."

Mary ran into her room. Everyone met at the door. "Well, let's go," said Mr. Smith. As there were getting into the car, Mr. Smith saw Mr. Johnson waved back.

Well I am sure he knows we are going to church.

At the church everyone got out, as they made the way to the church, the pastor spoke, "Good morning, Mr. and Mrs. Smith."

"Good morning, pastor." The kids had already gone inside.

As the Smiths entered the church, Mrs. Taylor said, "Hi, Windy, how are you?"

"Fine, how are and your family?"

"We are just fine. Two of our neighbor got saved."

"That is wonderful."

"Yes, they live across the street from us. The boy, his name is Roy. He and our son are friends. I met his mom yesterday. They are real nice people."

"That is so good," said Mrs. Taylor.

Well, it is time to start the service. So the ladies sat down. The service started off with singing. When the singing was over, the preacher began to talk.

"I want to welcome everyone to our church. When they pass the offering plate around, we have some cards that we would like for our visitors to fill one out. Just raise your hand, and we will give you one. We do have some things for our men to talk about. We need to get together this Wednesday to find out what to do. See brother Ted Williams after church. Have I missed anything?

"Pastor, the ladies have a meeting this Wednesday," said Sister Taylor.

"Okay, you all get together this Wednesday for that meeting Sister Taylor. Would you all turn your Bibles to Luke: 'We know that Jesus is coming soon. Jesus said as it was in the days of Noah so shall be days of his return. They did eat and drink, they married and given their marriage and brother and sisters that is what we are living in now. Jesus could come any day.'

"Now before I close, I want to give anyone a chance to make Christ the Lord, If not, we will close, be back Wednesday night. If I do not see you at the church, I will see in the rapture.

Brother Tom, would you say the word of prayer?"

"Dear Lord, I want to thank you for this service and your word be with us going home. We give you all the thanks, amen."

As they start to leave, Mrs. Smith said, "Pastor, have a good week."

"You all have a good week," said the pastor.

"Mom, do I have to go to school tomorrow?"

"Yes, Mary, Why?"

"Because I do not want to."

"Well you still have to."

When they got home, Steve said, "I see the Johnsons are still up."

"Yes, you are right, Steve."

"Mom, do you have any pie left over?"

"I think so Mary. Why you want some?"

"Yes, I would."

"Okay, get some plates out."

"Mom, I want a glass of milk," said Steve.

"Me too," said Mary.

"Okay, Mary, get some glass. Tom do you want anything?"

"No, I will watch a little TV, then go to bed. I have a big day tomorrow."

"Okay, honey. You know how the children are. When we come from church, they are ready to eat."

"Well, Mom, I have my homework done," said Steve.

"I know, son. You were doing your homework a couple of days ago."

"The service was good, wasn't it, Mom?" said Mary.

"Yes, honey."

"It was, the pastor is right."

"Yes, I think he is," said her mom.

The next day was Monday Mary hurried to get herself ready for school. Her mom was in the kitchen; her dad had left for work. He had to leave early. It was a little cold. Mary got her a jacket to wear.

"Mom, the weather is not right. It is a little cold when it supposed to be warm. Maybe it is because it was in the fall of the year, and it was the last of October but the weather was strange."

Mary hurried and got everything ready for school. Her books and her homework were at hand.

"Mom. I am ready."

"Young lady, you get your brother up. Tell him to come and eat and get ready for school."

"Okay, go eat. We have got to go to school."

"Mary come and eat," her mother said, as Mary sat down.

"Mom, did Dad leave early?"

"Yes, he did. He had an early job to do. Are you ready for school?"

"Yes, I am."

In comes Steve. "You sit down and eat," said his mom. "I made you eggs and toast, and glass of milk."

Then Mary and Steve get through eating. "Well, Mom, we are going to be late, if we do not hurry."

After the kids left, Mrs. Smith had work to do. "Well, I have got to get the wash done."

She began getting the clothes, putting them in the washer.

"Well, I have got to clean house, but first I need to read my Bible." She walked over to night stand, picked up tier Bible, and turned it to John. She was reading about Jesus coming back. This got her wonder what could happen real soon. I think I am going to read this tonight.

At the school Mary was looking at something and the teacher call her. "Mary what are you doing?"

Mary got up out of her seat, and she said, ".Jesus is coming." Mrs. Swill' said, "What did you say?" Mary said it again, "Jesus is coming,"

We know," said Mrs. Smith.

"No," said Mary, "I mean he is coming, you had better get ready." We will not have any more of your outburst."

"I mean it, Mrs. Smith."

"Well, you need to get your book on spelling. See if you can spell." "Okay, Mrs. Smith."

All the children looked at Mary. They began to talk, but Mary did not know what they were saying. After school, Mary went home. Her mother met her at the door.

"What happened at school today?"

"Mom, I had a strange felling come over me."

"Honey, you are so young to have things to come over you. You are only nine years old."

"But, Mom, I think Jesus wants

"Yes, I do."

"I think that is where it started; it could be."

"Well, Mary, if God wants you to work for him, he will let you know."

"Yes, Mom, I guess so."

"Where is your brother?"

"I think he is playing outside."

"Well, go tell him to change his clothes. He can wear them tomorrow."

"Okay, Mom."

As Mary went to the door, her friend starts to knock. "Hi, what are you are doing?" "My mom and I are going shopping. I want to know if you want to go."

"Let me call Steve first. Steve, Morn wants you."

"Okay, Mary, I am coming.

"She wants you to change clothes, so go to your room. Where are you going?"

"With my friend shopping, Mom, can I go with my friend and her mom shopping?"

"I guess so, but do not be gone too long. Your dad will be here soon, and we will be eating supper."

"Okay, Mom, let me get my jacket."

"Terry, Mary, come here."

"I will be right back, my morn wants me."

"Okay," said Terry, "I will wait in the car."

"What do you want, Mom?"

"Honey, you need to talk to your friend, Terry, about Jesus."

"Okay, Mom, I will."

"Remember, you hurry back."

"Bye, Mom."

"Bye, Mary."

"Terry, where are we going?"

"Mom wanted to go to grocer's store. She needs to get some meats and some more things. Do you need anything, Mary?"

"No, Mom bought groceries the other day. Terry, remember what we talked about that last day I saw you?"

"Yes."

"Well, have you been thinking about it?"

"Yes."

"You know Jesus is coming soon."

"I know. That is what my Granny Jones told me. I used to go to church with her. She is a true Christian woman."

"Is she your dad's mom?"

"Yes, she is. She has talked to me many times."

"What about your mom?"

"She don't say anything."

"Does she believe in Jesus?"

"I do not know. But if something happened, I would go to Granny Jones. And if she gone, I would cry."

"Why don't you give your heart to God, then you won't be left behind."

"Really?"

"Yes, I am telling you the truth."

"I need to have some time before I do it."

"Okay, but when it happens, you won't go. You may not have any time."

"Terry, where are you?" called her mother.

"Here I am," said Terry.

"Well, I am ready to check out."

"Terry, I hope you change your mind."

"I do not know."

"Well, girls, let's go," said Mrs. Jones. "Mary, do you want to go over to the house and play with Terry?" asked Mrs. Jones.

"No, Mom told me to come back home as soon as we get back."

"Okay, here are you."

"Bye, Terry and Mrs. Jones."

"Bye, Mary, if you every want to come over just call me, and I will come and pick you up."

"Okay, Mrs. Jones."

When Mary got out, she said, "See you later, Terry. Remember what I told you."

"Okay, I will."

As they pulled off, Mrs. Jones asked, "What was Mary talking about, Terry?"

"I will tell you later."

"No, I want you to tell me now."

"Okay, Morn, she was talking about Jesus."

"What about him?"

"She said he was coming soon."

"Well, honey, before your Granny Smith passed away, she was talking to me about Jesus coming."

"Morn, was that your mom?"

"Yes, honey she was. She passed before you were born. You never met her. She was real sick, and God took her. I was with her when she left this world. She asked me if I saw angels in her room."

"She did, Morn?"

"Yes, honey. So I know without a doubt where your Granny Smith is. She was a good woman who loves the Lord. She took us to church.

"Mom, you never told me about her."

"I know but when we get home, I will you show you pictures of her and your Grandfather Smith. They both are in heaven. I think."

"What happened to you, Mom? I never heard you talk about Jesus."

"Why I do not know. But that is going to change. I know your granny prayed for my brothers and sisters. Now we are here at the house. Let's get out and go in. I will show you pictures."

"Okay, Mom."

"Here is my picture; this is your granny and me when I was seven years old."

"Your mom was pretty."

"Yes, I think so."

"Now here is one of your granny and Grandpa Smith."

"Mom, you look like both of them."

"You think so? They were real young in this picture. But they were married."

"Mom, what about Dad? Does he knows Jesus?"

"Honey, he does not talk about him. But your Granny Jones, she took him to church."

"She did, Mom?"

"Yes, well, maybe he does know. We will see."

"You know, Mom, all of Mary's family are Christians, her dad, her mother, and brother. The little boy that lives across the street he got saved. Mary's brother, Steve, led him in a sinner prayer."

"Really?"

"Terry, that is what Mary said."

"Okay, well that is good."

"Mom, do you think Jesus is coining'?"

"Well that is what your granny said before she passed.

"He could come tonight, Mom'?"

"Yes, he could. I think we need to lied us another church."

"Why, Mom? Don't you like our church'?"

"Yes, honey, but it does not Preach on the rapture. And if your Granny Smith had not told me, I would never know."

"Sorry, Mom."

"That is okay, honey. Now I need to put these pictures up and fix supper."

Back at Mary's mom. "You home'?"

"Yes, Mom."

"Did you get to talk to your friend'?"

"Yes, Mom."

"Well what happened?"

"Nothing, she did not say anything yet, Mom, but it was as before."

"Well, honey you need to pray for your friend."

"I will. Mom, is Dad in yet?"

"No, honey, he is a little late. I am making supper. It will be done by the time he gets home.

"Mom, do you think Terry will be okay?"

"Mary, tonight when you pray, say a special one for Terry. God does answer prayers."

"I know he does, Mom. Mom, I heard Dad, he just pulled up in the yard."

"Mary, tell your brother to come in. It is time to eat."

"Okay, Mom. Steve, come in."

About that time her dad came in. "Steve your mom wants you," said his dad.

"Okay, Dad, I am coming."

"How was your day, Tom?"

"Okay, I did have lots to do. That is why I am late. But I can see that you made my favorite supper."

"Yes, I did. I hope you like it."

"Well, I am real tired, but I can eat something."

"Dad, are we still going fishing Saturday?"

"Yes, son, if Mr. Johnson wants to go, and I am sure he does. I will go over to his house Friday after work and see if he still wants to go."

"Okay, Dad"

"Now you get here and eat. Your mom made us a good supper, and we also have our family get-together tonight."

"Yes. Mary, before you sit down, go into my bedroom and get my Bible,"

"Here it is, Mom."

"Okay, put it on the table in the living room."

So that is what Mary did. "Tom, are you going, to talk to Mr. Johnson about the rapture?"

"I was thinking about it. We can all pray for that family."

"Is every one finished?"

"Yes, I think so," said her husband.

"Everyone, go to the living room."

"Okay, Mom," said Mary.

"I will be there when I get the table cleaned off."

"Mom, what are you reading tonight'?"

"Well, Mary, I will start out talking about God's word. So you all just sit down, and I will get everything taken care of real fast."

It took Mrs. Smith about ten minutes, and she was finished.

"Okay, Jesus died for us all, that is how much he loved us, and his strips were for our healing. He took up on that cross our sins. When he came to the earth, he healed the sick and the blind, he opened their eyes. Many things he did, he wanted the best for us. My mother told me many times things would happen in her childhood, days that her mother would pray for them, and God would heal them. They were very poor. So she depended on God to get them thought hard times. So kids, I have never told you about when I was young. My mom and dad went through lots before they got any money."

"So, Mom, you were poor?"

"Yes, I was. My dad was working for himself, and his job was lots of people work there."

"Did your mom work?"

"No, she had plenty to do in our home, like taking care of us kids. There were six of us kids, and Mom had to cook for us while Dad worked. This was the time when things were not easy to get things. Dad worked hard, and it took most of it take care of our family. Well, you kids, time to pray. Let's remember the Johnsons, and Terry and her family."

"Yes, Mom, I will say a special pray for Terry,"

The phone rang. "Mary, would you get that?"

"Yes, Mom. Hello."

"Mary, this is Terry."

"Yes, Terry."

"Remember what you were talking about?"

"Yes."

"Well I told my mom, and we want to go to your church."

What did your mom say?"

"Well, I told my mom, and we want to go church."

"What did your mom say?"

"Well, it seems as though her mom told her about Jesus. And Mom wants to change churches because they do not believe in the rapture."

"Good. Are your going Sunday?"

"Yes, that is when Mom wants to go."

"You all can sit with us."

"That will be good."

"I will tell Mom and Dad. We will look for you all."

"What is your mom's name?"

"Windy Smith. We will see you all the church."

"Mom, that was Terry."

"What did she want?"

"She and her mom want to go to church."

"When do they want to go?"

"Sunday."

"Well, that is good. Now let's pray. Tom, how about you praying,for our family?"

"Dear Lord, I want to thank you for your love and blood you shed on that cross for us. Lord, we want to remember the Johnsons, help them to walk in the right way. Bless them, Lord, and also Terry's family, my daughter's friend. They have made up the mind to trust in you, love you, Lord, amen."

"Okay, you all can watch TV for a little. There's school tomorrow. Do you both have homework?"

"I do. Mom." said Mary.

"Okay, get to it. Good night to you both."

"Good night. Mom and Dad," said Mary. "See you in the morning."

"Do not forget to pray."

The next morning is Wednesday. Mary got up shortly after waking up to go school early. Her mom heard her as she came to the kitchen.

"What do you want for breakfast?"

"Mom. I will have one egg and toast."

"While I get it ready. get your brother up."

"Okay. Mom. Steve, get up and get ready for school."

"Okay, Mary, see you in the kitchen."

"When Mary went back to the kitchen, her mother asked, "Is Steve up yet?"

"Yes. Mom, he is coming."

"Okay. Steve you eat your breakfast."

"Mom, did Dad leave early?"

"Yes. he leaves early every morning this week."

"I hope he isn't too tired to go fishing."

"You mean Saturday?"

"Yes, Mom, that is when we plan on going."

"He will be okay, when it comes to going fishing, also he wants to witness to Mr. Johnson. I hope he is okay with what your father has to say."

Johnson. I hope he is okay with what your father has to say."

"Me too, Mom."

"Well it is time to go to school. You both have a good day." Their mom kissed them on the face. "You too, Mom," said Mary.

When Mary got outside, she saw Roy coming out of their door.

"Mary, I am going to walk to school with Roy."

"Okay, I will see you there. Now do not lag behind. Do not be late. We have an early day, we will get out early.

"I know I will go over to Roy's to play when I get home, if it is okay with Mom."

Mary walked on to school. She saw her friend Becky. "Hi, how are you? Are you going to church tonight?"

"I guess."

"Are you and your family?"

"Mom did say something about it, so I guess so. Well, if Dad works late we will not be going. He has been working late every night this week."

Well, it is time to go to on our room."

"Yes, it is. I wonder where Steve is at."

"I do not see him," said Mary.

After school, when Mary got home, she called, "Mom."

"Yes, Mary"

"Do you think Dad will be home early?"

"No, why?"

"Because I saw Becky at school, and she wanted to know if we were going to church tonight."

"I do not think so because your dad is going to be real late. Is that Granny Stone's granddaughter?"

"Yes, Mom. Becky goes to our church with her granny. Her mom and dad don't go. Why, I don't know. I just saw Granny stone and Becky. I do not know Becky's mom and dad."

In came Steve. "Mom, can I go and play with Roy?"

"For a little. When it gets dark you come home."

"Okay, Mom," Steve said, "see you in a little while, Mom."

"Okay, son, do you have any homework?"

"No, Mom, the teacher Mrs. Perry did not give us any homework."

"Okay, you go on and play. When you see your father coming, you come home."

"I will."

"Mary, you get my Bible so we can have our family get-together after supper."

"Okay, Mom, where is it at?"

"On my dresser where I left it."

"Here it is, Mom."

"Mary, I have a story to tell you about my Bible."

"What, Mom?"

"Do you know how I got my Bible?"

"No, but it looks real old."

"It is, honey. Your Grandmother Jones gave it to me. She asked me what I wanted for my birthday when I was twelve years old. And this was her Bible. She had this when she was twelve, and I wanted it. I ask her for it when I was ten years old. She could not give it to me then. Mom got sick, and she came to me at my birthday and that is what she gave me because she knew I wanted it. So this Bible will go to you if anything happens to me."

"Thank you, Mom. Look, Mom, it has something written in it."

"Yes, honey it does. It is how your grandmother got it. So this is history to you."

"Mom, I see the car lights of Dad's car."

"Are you sure?"

"Yes, here comes Steve."

"Where have you been?" asked his dad.

"I was over at Roy, my friend's house."

"Okay, did you tell your mom?"

"Yes. I did."

"How was your day?" said his wife inside.

"Okay. I guess. You know we missed Wednesday night service."

Yes. but we will be able to go next Wednesday. I know sometimes we cannot go.

Well. I have supper done, we will be able to have our family get-together when we have our supper. I have my Bible here. Mary, take into the living room."

"Okay, Mom, now let's eat."

"What is going on with your friend, Steve?" said his mom.

"Well, he is happy to go fishing Saturday. We talked about that, and he is glad to be saved, living for the Lord. He has not told his dad yet, only his mom. And, Mom, he wants to go to our church Sunday."

"Okay, he can go with us. If he wants to."

"I think so. Mom."

"Now let's eat. How was your day, Mary?"

"Okay, Dad we got out early from school."

"That was nice, said her dad."

"We get out early every Wednesday. I like that."

"Yes. I think you do. Well everyone, time to read the Bible. I am reading from Revelation chapter 12 verse 9: 'and the great dragon was cast out that old serpent called the devil which deceiveth the whole world he was cast out into the earth. And his angels were cast out with him. Now when Jesus comes back, the old devil will be in change for one thousand years."

"Why, Mom? said Mary.

"Because he is so trying to be better than God and that will never happen. Okay, Mary, will you pray for the family?"

"Yes. Mom, 'Dear Lord thanks for the day, thank you for my family, and Lord keep us in your will, amen."

"Okay, you all we can watch a little TV and then to bed we go.

Thursday morning came early. Mary ran into the kitchen. "Mom, where are you at'?"

"Honey, here I am."

"Mom, I would like some eggs and toast."

"I thought you would. Go get your breakfast; it is on the stove ready for you."

"Well, Mom we are still here."

"Yes, we are. Why would you say that?"

"Mom, I had a dream last night. Jesus came back. I woke from my sleep. Then, I put my feet on the floor. And I heard the trumpet sound, it was so loud, and then I felt myself moving in the air, at that time I saw Jesus, he was so beautiful I could not see his face, it was glowing like a light, and the angels were with him, they were all in white. I felt so much love. I could see the people from earth meting Jesus, and all were changed like the Bible said. Mom, I was so happy to see him. You know, Mom, you said I had never seen my Granny Smith. Well, I feel like I saw her. Mom, did she have long gray hair?"

"Yes, Mary she did, and I remember a mole on her face."

"But, Mom, that cannot be right. Maybe Jesus wanted me to see her because it was a dream and it seemed so real."

"Honey, where was the mole at?"

"In the middle of her head."

"That is true, she did have one there. That is strange that you would dream about your granny." "Well, I did then. In my dream we were going to heaven, and I woke up. It seemed so real, Mom."

"Well, it is going to come to pass soon."

"I will be happy, Mom."

"Well you get ready for school. Get your brother up. I do not want you all to be late."

"Did dad leave already, Mom?"

"No, honey, he had to go to the store."

"Is he going to work?"

"Yes, he will be a little late."

"Here he comes now, Mom.

"Good, you go get ready for school. You have only two more days before the weekend." In walks Mr. Smith. "Here, I bought a tub of butter. We were out."

"Good, I am glad you pick it up. I do need to go grocery shopping soon. Mary, go get your brother up now."

"Okay, Mom."

"Well, our little girl had the most extraordinary dream."

"What did she say it was?" said her husband.

"She dreamed Jesus came. She said it seemed so real. She also told me she saw Mom. And, honey, I believe her because she told me about the mole Mom had. Do you remember where it was?"

"I think it was in the middle of her head."

"That is right. And that is what Mary told me. She said had long gray hair."

"Yes, she did."

"Well how do you think Mary would know that if it wasn't true? She never saw Mom."

"Well that is something," said her husband.

"Mary wanted to tell me that before she went to school."

"Steve, are you up?" Mary called out.

"Yes."

"Get ready for school, and mom has you some breakfast in the stove."

"Well, I have got to go," said her husband. "I will get home early, so I can go over and talk to James about fishing."

"I thought you were going over Friday"

"Well, I will do it today when I get home. See you kids." He leaned over and kissed his wife goodbye, and he was gone. Out comes Mary.

"I am leaving, Mom, for school. Come on, Steve, let's go."

"Hold on, let me finish my milk."

"Okay, but you hurry. Roy has already gone. I saw him leave early out the door."

They both go. "Bye, kids."

"See you all after school, Mom."

Just right then, her mind was on the reading of God's word: The devil in chained where he will not be of brother to God's people. The dream she had-the one she told her mom about. She knew she had to listen on the teacher, Mrs. Smith. She said to herself, "I need to think of this when I get home; my schooling means a lot to me. Today is Thursday. I have one more day till the weekend comes."

She wanted to pray about what God wanted her to go. Maybe he wanted her to talk to the kids about his son coming. She was thinking about Terry wanting to go to church Sunday with them. She was so happy. "I will pray for her," she said to herself. She had lots of work at school.

Mrs. Smith was getting things ready for their get-together after supper. "I will put my Bible on the TV stand so it will be at my fingertips. I will pray before the kids come home. 'Dear Lord, be with us the rest of the week. Be with my husband as he and our son go fishing with their friends Saturday. Put words in his mouth, what he should say to help him to lead Mr. Johnson to you, amen.'"

When Mrs. Smith got up, she saw Mrs. Johnson coming to visit her. "Hi, Mrs. Smith, how are you?"

"I am okay."

"Fine, do you have a minute?"

"Sure, come on in. What can I help you with? Mrs. Smith said, adding, "Hold that thought. I have tea. Would you like some?"

"Yes, thank you."

"What was it you wanted?"

"It is my husband."

"I am sorry, Mrs. Johnson, no need to be formal. Can I call you Mary? My name, is Windy

Now that we know each other's name, what were you saying about your husband? Mary, hold that though, I have some fresh tea. Would you like some?"

"Yes, thank you. I was telling you about my husband. His name is James."

"Yes, my husband is Tom. Now that we have the names okay, what was it you wanted to talk about?"

"It's my husband. He does not believe in God. He has made my life really bad."

"Well my husband and son, his name is Steve, are so happy to go fishing Saturday with your husband and son. Do not worry about your husband. My husband will be glad to talk to him about Jesus."

"Good, I hope so."

"Has your husband told you about the trip?"

"No, well, maybe he will tonight. He has been busy."

"What you need to do is pray for him. Your son told us he did not tell his dad he got saved. He said he told you.

"That is true. Roy does help me."

"He said he tried to help you. The first night he was at our house, he listened to me read the Bible, and it was the night he got saved. He was an open the book. I guess he wanted to tell someone what he had bottled up in him. He wanted so much to hear about Jesus. Mary we are having Roy a birthday party. You will he welcome."

Mrs. Johnson said, "I have got to go. My son will he home soon. We will talk later. I want to thank you so much."

Then Mary left. Mrs. Smith went back into the house. She thought she heard Mary, her daughter. "Mary is that you?"

"Yes, Mom, it is. I have got to put my books up. I will be there in a little."

"You will find me in the kitchen."

"Mom, I had lot on my mind. At school, it had something to do with my dream. Remember, I told you about my dream?"

"Yes, I remember."

"When I was at school, it all came back. I could not think. I just wanted to get my mind on school. That is what I did.

"Honey, I think God is letting us know things in our dreams that he is coming soon."

"Mom, was that Mrs. Johnson coming from our house?"

"Yes, honey, it was. She had lots of things on her mind. She wanted to talk to me." "What was it about, Mom?"

"Mary, you know she is saved?"

"You told me that, Mom"

"Honey, her husband does not believe in God. It is hard for Mrs. Johnson. She cannot deal with it. She asked me what to do."

"What did you tell her Mom?"

"I told her to pray for him. That is what I would have told her. God is the answer when you frighten a nonbeliever. Maybe Dad can get him to change his mind on that fishing trip.

"Mom, I have homework."

"Mary, where is Steve?"

"In the yard playing, I think."

"Tell him to come in the house. Your dad is coming home early."

"Mom what do you want?"

"Do you have homework to do?"

"A little. Our teacher, Mrs. Smith did not have time to give us any. She was late for a meeting."

"Go to your and do it."

"Mom."

"Yes, Steve."

"What do I wear Saturday?"

"You have got some long pants in the closet, and you can wear your boots if you are going to be in the woods. And you will need some long socks. You will not wear your church clothes. I will get your clothes and what you need for trip. When you get home from school, they will be ready."

"Okay, Mom. Now I will do my homework. Mom, here comes Dad. He is early."

"Hi, Windy, what have you been doing."

"I had company."

"Who?"

"Mrs. Johnson, she stopped by."

"She did?"

"Yes, she wanted to talk to me about her husband."

"What is going on? Is it because he has a new family?"

"Yes, he has been mean to her."

"Why? He was nice to me."

"You did not go there to preach to him. You may have a different point of view after your fishing trip. I will be praying for you."

"What did you tell her?"

"I told her to pray about it."

"That would be what I would say. Honey, I have go to get a shower. I will be going over to see Mr. Johnson. I have things I have got to do Friday. I guess he is still wanted to go. Windy, honey, can you find me some clothes to wear?"

"Yes, I am going to get Steve some clothes, so I will look for you some too."

Tom you sure got Steve's spirits high. He wants to go so bad. I think he will have a good time. "Windy, since I got my shower, I am going over to James."

"Be back by six," said Windy.

"I see you then," said her husband.

"Are you going to speak about Jesus?"

"Not until Saturday."

"When you get back, supper will be done."

When Mary walked by Steve's room, she said, "Steve, are you happy to go fishing Saturday?"

"Yes, Mary, I will be; I can't wait. It has been a while since I have been anywhere."

"Have you finished your homework?"

"I hope I can go over to play with Roy."

"You had better go and ask Mom."

Steve went to the kitchen. "Mom, can I go over to play with Roy?"

"Not now, that is where your dad is. Wait until your dad comes back."

"Dad is there?"

"Yes, he is. He wanted to talk to Mr. Johnson. It is about the plans going fishing Saturday."

"We will have a good time."

"I think so," said his mom. "Is Mary still working on her homework?"

"I think she has almost finished."

"Okay, I need for her to come to the kitchen."

Mary heard her mom. "I will be there in a minute."

When Tom got to the Johnsons, he knocked at the door. James answered. "How are you? Come on in. I was watching a little TV. It was some of them old movies. Do you ever watch the old movies?"

"Sometimes I do, I came over to see if our fishing plans were still on?"

"Yes, it is. I have been looking forward to Saturday."

"Me too," said Tom.

"I would like to take the boat out," said James.

"That would be nice," said Tom.

"I was coming over Friday, but something came up. That changed my mind."

"Well, I had something to do myself," said James. "I need to get the boat ready. It is at my brother's. I need to call him, let him know that I will pick it up."

"You know. I was thinking about you needed a job. They have an opening where I work if you want to apply."

"Where do you work at?"

"Sears. I have been there ten years. My boss is a good friend of ours, and if I ask him, he will give you a job."

"What part do you work at?"

"I sell tires. We need another salesman. Do you think you could do it?"

"I did work at Walmart. I was selling shoes. It has been a while."

"I will remind myself to get you application so you can fill it out. It has been open for a while. That is why I have work a lot of hours. The guy that worked there moved out of state. He did not give us any time to get someone else."

"I sure hope it is still open," said James.

"Yes, you can ride with me should you go to work."

"That is nice. We can help each other."

"Well. James, I promised Windy I would be home by six to eat."

"What time do you want to leave Saturday?" said James.

"Well, I was thinking around five would be good, since we are taking the boat. How far is the fishing hole?"

"About one mile."

"That is not too far."

"Could you go to work Monday?"

"If they still need someone, I will."

"Okay, my wife would be happy. She has been working for some time. It would give her a break. She is not able to work. If I go back to work, she could rest. I will tell her that tonight. My son's is birthday soon. I would like to get him something nice. He is getting to be young man. He has changed since he has been around you all."

"James we will talk later. I promised Windy I would be home by six. She said supper would be ready."

Tom left. When he got home, he could smell his wife's supper. "Wow that smells good."

"Glad you think so."

"I told James about the opening at work. I think they will hire him."

"You do?"

Well, I sure hope so. I think he would be a good worker. And I am going to help him to get it."

"That is good," said his wife. "Supper is done. Are you ready to eat? Will you be leaving early in the morning?"

"Yes, I want to get everything finished by the weekend. Sit down, and I will make you a plate. Mary you and you brother come and eat. Your dad is here."

We have our Bible studies tonight, do not forget. Mom what are you going to read us?" Replied Mary, "What about Mark, chapter 14, verse 20,"

"Okay, Mom, anything about Jesus?"

"Yes, Mary. He is what our lives are about. He is what my family is about. He is why we are living. He is the reason I get up in the morning. He gets me up. Mary, he is coming soon. I want to get many ready for that day."

'Yes, Mom, he could come tonight."

"Everyone, it is time for our family to get together. We can start our Bible reading."

"Mom, do you want me to help you with the dishes?"

"No, I will do them later. Does anyone want a special prayer?"

"We have lots we need to remember when we pray," said Mary, "the Johnson and my friend."

"What I am going to read to you was the cross of Jesus. This is when they went to break bread with Jesus. Jesus told them the one that betrayed him was one of his twelve that dipped with him in the dish. The son of man indeed goeth as it is written of him. But woe to that man by whom, the son of man is betrayed good were it for that man if he had never been born.' You see, family, Jesus had bread and wine before he was put to death, and two of his disciples, the devil, was in them. This was what Jesus was telling them that he knows what they would do. Peter denied him. Judas betrayed him."

"Why?" said Mary. How could they be so mean to Jesus?"

"I do not know, Mary, but they were. He prayed to the Father to remove the cup from him."

"What cup, Mom?" said Steve. "I do not understand."

It was the cup of sorrow from all of his people. That is why it says in the Bible, we all have sin come short of the glory of God. That is what the preacher said. You are right, son. Tom, we need for you to lead us in pray so we can get ready for bed."

"Dear Lord, thank you for your word and the blood you shed for all of us and the blessings you have given us. Have your way in the Johnsons' lives, and Lord, Mary's friend, Terry, lead her to you, amen."

"Kids time to watch a little TV before bed time."

"Mom, Jesus loves us?"

"Yes, Mary, he does."

The night was short. Mary got up and ran to the kitchen. "Mom, we are still here."

"What is wrong? Did you have one of your dreams?"

"No, Mom, I just feel that way. I know it will not be long. The people do not care what happen anymore."

"Mary, get your brother up. Don't forget, it is Friday. We got one week till the end of October, then we have a birthday party to plan. Mary. do you know what the date is?"

"I think it is the eighth of November. Christmas is so close. What are we planning to do?"

"Well, we will put some things on layaway. I want to get your dad something special. I know Dad will like that. Mary, are you ready for school?

"I am leaving now, Mom. I will get Steve up. I hope lie is up already. I will check. Mom, has Dad left yet?"

"Yes, he left early this morning. But I look for him home early than before. He wants to get things ready for fishing. I will get their clothes ready for them so they can get on the road. They want to leave around 5:00 a.m. They are taking James's boat. And they cannot go too fast."

"Here is Steve now, Mom; he wants a glass of milk."

"I am not hungry, Mom."

"Not coming down with something, are you Steve?"

"No, Mom," I am okay.

"I do not want to be late for school, Mom."

"I am going, come on, Steve. I want to see Becky before time for school. She will be there early."

"Okay, Mary, I am coming. Bye, Mom, see you this afternoon."

"Bye kids. You all have a good day."

"Mom, do not forget my clothes. I am ready for my fishing trip. Wait, Mary, you are walking too fast."

"Come on, Steve, hurry. I do not want to be late at school." Mary saw her friend. Becky. "I'm waiting on you. I did get here early," said Becky. I had to go shopping with Granny Stone."

"Flow is she doing?" said Mary.

"She is okay, I guess. She is looking forward going to church Sunday. She loves to go to church. "I see the kids going into the rooms," said Mary. "We had better go; do not want to be late." Mary was not too good at spelling, and she knew it was one of her subjects for the day.

The day went fast; no homework Mary was very happy that there was no homework.

"See everyone Monday," said their teacher. Mary went to get her brother. She saw him in his room.

"Come on, Steve. Let's go."

"Go on, I will catch up with you."

"You had better come on."

On her way home, she saw Roy not to upset leaving Steve by himself.

When Mary got home, she was out of breath. "What is wrong with you?" asked her mother.

"I ran all the way from school."

"Where is your brother at?"

"You know, Mom, how boys are. He will be along later. I think he is with Roy. Because on the way here, I saw Roy. He was going to Steve's room."

"Honey, when Jesus was twelve years old, he went to the temple to preach God's word. His mother, Mary, and lather were looking for him. When they found him, he told them he was about his Father's work."

"Okay, Mom, so Jesus did a lot for his people?"

"Yes, he did. Now, it is getting late and your dad will get up early."

"Okay, Mom, see you in the morning. You too, Dad."

"Good night, Mary," said her dad.

"Steve, it is time to go to bed."

"I am going, Mom.

"Okay, when it is time to get up, don't let me hear anything out of your mouth. I have got to go too," said his dad.

"I will be there in a little while," said his wife. "I need to get up early myself."

The next morning came early. Windy heard the clock go off. "Come on, Tom, hit the floor. My goodness, it sure went fast."

"Windy, will you go get Steve up?"

"Okay. Steve, get up, time to rise and shine, are you up?"

"Yes, Mom, I am."

"Your dad is up already. He is getting ready. I am going to make you and your dad sandwich.""Mom, do not forget Roy and his dad."

"Okay, won't."

While Windy was in the kitchen, in came Mary. "Honey you are up too early. You need to lie back down. It is 5:00 a.m. too early for you.

Your dad and brother are leaving early so they can get a good start. They are taking Mr. Johnson's boat."

In walked Steve. "Here I am, Mom. Mary, why are you up?"

"I am on my way back to the bed."

In walked Tom. "Well, I am going to be warm."

"I am glad," said his wife.

"Steve, it is time to go. Are you ready? said his dad.

"Did you get your coffee?" said his wife.

"I did. Windy. can you find me something to put it in? So it will not leak."

"Here I found you a cup. It is okay."

"Let's go Steve, we need to get on the road."

"Bye, Mom."

"You have a good day fishing with the Johnsons."

"Tom kissed his wife. "We will be back soon, I hope. I am a little sleepy."

"You sure you want to go?"

"Yes, I need to talk to James about Jesus."

"I see," said his wife.

"I will see you later."

And tom and Steve left. When they were at James's house, Tom knocked on the door.

James came to the door.

"Are you ready James?" asked Tom.

"Yes, I am. Let me see if Roy is ready. I put the boat on the car last night."

Out to the truck, they all go. Dad, I will get the poles out," said Steve. "Okay, son did you think of bringing Roy one of your poles?"

"Yes, Dad, I have it here."

"James, has Roy ever used one of these poles like this?"

"Yes, he has, but a few months ago. We went to the ocean in Florida. At that time, he borrowed one from his friend. It was real long. My son had a hard time using it. It looks like that one. Well. It is time to go, guys."

"We are ready," replied Tom. As they were leaving, Tom asked, "How many people do you ever see at this place?"

"Not too many since it cold."

"I guess you have your favorite place that you fish it?" said Tom.

"Yes, I do, but today we have the boat. And we will be away out in the water."

"You have a nice boat."

"I think so too," said Roy.

"I bet you are happy to go fishing with your dad?"

"Yes, sir, you are right. I know Steve likes going. Can you swim?"

"No, sir."

"Well. I did not know that," said his dad. "I thought they taught that in school. Maybe, I do not know. Well, you had better stay from the water. I will keep an eye on you. Your mom will be all over me."

"I will be okay, Dad."

"Do you need to stop at the store, Tom?"

"Windy made us all sandwich, so we are okay."

"Please thank Windy for the sandwich."

"Well. I need to stop at the store. It is just up the road, and I will pick us up some drinks to c'a with the sandwich that Windy made us."

"Well we are here. Do you boys need anything?"

"No, Dad, we are good."

"Well. I made it through the line." He put the drinks in the boat. For that to be a small store, they sure had a lot of customers. I thought I was going to stay in that lane. Someone felt sorry for me and let me in front of them."

"That is good." said Tom. "Sorry you had a bad time in the store."

"It is okay. Well, we made it everybody out. Now we can push the boat over there at the dock; good place to go in."

"Dad, do you want me to put the drinks in the truck?" asked Roy.

"Yes, Roy, that would be nice. After we fish a while, we will drink some. Tom brought some nice sandwich his wife made us."

"Cool, dad."

"Is everyone ready to go fishing? Get the poles and put them in the boat, Steve."

"Can I help?" said Roy.

"Okay, you can get the one I brought you. Dad, here is yours. I will put them where we can find them." said Steve. "Roy, bring them here so they will all be together. Roy, you come here and sit by me so I can see what you are doing."

"I will catch a big one when I get my worm on my hook," said Roy.

"Dad, where is the bait?"

"It is in the back of the bait. You sit down; it will still be there when we stop the boat. I do not want you to tall overboard"

"Dad I will be okay."

No one was watching Roy when he decided to go to the hack of the boat. Ills dad was talking to Tom. "You know, Tom. When I came out here one day, I got me a big catfish. It weighed at least five pounds or more."

"What did you do with it, James?"

"I put it back into the water."

"Why?"

"Because it was so yellow."

"What—there is nothing wrong with that.

"Really, Tom?"

"Well, I have seen them at the market before, and they are selling them. Look, James, you have a bite."

"Yes, a small one," he said.

James noticed Roy was gone. "Roy, where are you? I need bait. Roy, did you hear me? James did not want to think where his son was. He told him to stay put now he is gone. "Where is that boy at?" he asked.

Steve began to look; he is not in the boat. James was looking out in the water. There he is, as he jumped into the water. He heard Roy calling him. "Help me," said Roy, with a chilling scream. "Please help me." His dad was getting closer. Roy was still calling to his dad when he went under the water.

"Oh my Lord," cried Tom, as he jumped into the water as Roy went down again. James pulled him back up. By that time, Tom had made it to where they were at.

"Come on, Roy," his dad said with tears in his eyes.

"I have a phone in the truck. Tom, call 911, please. We need help."

Tom rushed to the truck. He grabbed the phone. With trembling hands, Tom dialed 911.

"911 Ambulance, this is Peggy Stone, can I help you?"

"We have a boy here that fell overload. We need an ambulance to come to 63 Street off of Creek Road; hurry."

"Is the boy talking?"

"No he is not. Lady, would you please get someone here now?"

"We have someone coming your way. Try to keep him warm so he won't go into shock. Have you tried CPR?"

"I do not know. His dad is with him. Let me go. I see the ambulance. Okay, bye."

"You want me to pray for Roy?"

"Yes, I do. I do not want to lose my son."

The paramedic began to ask what Roy name was. His dad answered and told them what happened: "Well, to put short, my son fall into the water."

Before they left, James said, "Can you tell me how he is?"

Well, we have checked him out. It looks like he is in a coma."

"What?" said his dad.

"He is not talking to us. We cannot say what is going in until we check him out at the hospital." "Go on James get in with your son. We will take your truck and boat home. We will put it at your house. I will give the keys to your wife."

"My wife is not home."

"Okay, when you all come home, everything will be at my house."

"Thank you, Tom."

"Let us know how Roy is."

"I will."

When James got into the ambulance, he sat by his son, brushed back his brown hair, and the tears began to fall on his son's face. He could hear Tom saying we will be praying for him.

James also saw his son hooked up to an IV. It made him want to pray. "Dear Lord, I did not believe in you at one time. I am so sorry for my sins. Please forgive me. Do not let my son die. If this happened because of my sins, please Lord, I will do anything."

At that moment, James felt peace. He could not understand what was going on inside of him. He felt love like he had not felt before, then he saw an angel over his son. He knew his son was going to be okay. He began to thank God. The tears began to come down. He said to himself, "My son is going to be okay." When they got to the hospital, James got out. A nurse asked him to follow her. She needs him to tell her Roy's name, age, and other things.

"What is your son's name?"

"Roy Gene Johnson. My name is James Johnson."

"Do you know what happened to your son?"

"Just he fell into the water. About an hour before it happened, I found out he could not swim, so I told him to sit by me, and I guess he got up, and that is when it happened. He was with me one minute and gone the next. I put my pole in the water and I caught a fish. I missed my son. When I called for him; that is when I saw him. He was in the water fighting for his life. I jumped in and got to him when he went the second time. I heard his chilling scream. I was so scared."

"Do you have insurance?"

"Yes, I do. Here is my card. Here is all you will need about my son. He will be eleven in two weeks. His birthday is soon."

In walked the doctor. "Nurse, could you leave the room. I need to talk to Roy's parents. Mr. and Mrs. Smith, I am Dr. King."

"How is our son?" said Mrs. Johnson.

"Well, he has come out of the coma. It was something we do not understand, what happened to your son. He was out and then he is talking."

"Can we see him, doctor?"

"Sure, Come in."

"Where did you come from?"

"Well, James, I work here when they brought Roy in. I came here. I did not see you, but Roy was not talking."

"Okay we will talk later. Here he is."

The Rapture of the Church

"Dad, Mom." They both ran to their son." "Son, are you okay?" said his dad.

"Yes, I am."

"You people spend some time with your son. I will be in tomorrow to see how he is doing."

"Dad, I saw Jesus."

"What?"

"He put his hand on me, and I felt peace. Dad, don't you believe me?"

"Yes, son I do. I also had an encounter with some angels when they were bringing you to the hospital. Son, I have a confession."

"What Dad?"

"Well, I prayed for you, and I gave my heart to God."

"Dad, that is so good. Mom, don't you think so?"

"So you believe in God now?"

"Yes, son, I guess almost losing you woke me up. And you know, son, I am glad God took control."

"Dad, I am so glad you gave your heart to God."

"Me too," said his mom.

They were all happy. "Now we can all go to heaven when the rapture takes place. Son, your mom and I are going to get some coffee. Can we bring you anything back?"

"No, Dad, I will rest while you and mom are gone."

Back to Tom and his family. "Steve, when we get home, we will put James's truck and boat at the house."

"Dad, I wonder how Roy is doing."

"Well, son, I think he is okay."

"Me too, Dad, I will call the hospital when I get to the house. Dad, where do you want to put the boat?"

"Over there will be okay. I see your mom's home. Her car is in the driveway."

As Tom got out of the car, his wife met him at the door. "What are you doing with James truck and boat?"

"Honey, it is so bad. Thank God, he was there.

"What are you saying?" said Windy.

"James's son, Roy, fell into the water."

"What?"

"Well, you know we went fishing."

"Yes, well, Roy was sitting by his dad, and Steve was sitting with me as we were fishing.

All at once Roy went missing."

"What happened? Is he okay?"

"He is okay. His dad got to him before he went down the last time. He is in the hospital.

"Wow I feel sorry for his mom was she there?"

"Yes, that is where she works at. I need to call and check up on him now. He was in a coma. I do not know how he is."

"That is bad," said his wife.

"I told James we would pray for him."

"Sure we will."

"Windy, will you get me the numbers? So I can call. He is in room 202, second floor, children's ward."

"Honey, I will look for it." Windy got the phone book.

"Here it is. Tom."

"Hand me the phone. I will call."

"Okay, the number ... Tom calls." Hello, this is Orange Hospital. My name is Mrs. Green. Can I help you?"

"Yes. I need room 202, second floor, please. Okay, it is ringing. Hello, is this room 202?"

"Yes, who is this?"

"This is Tom Smith."

"You are speaking to James, Tom."

"How is Roy doing?"

"Well, Tom, you may not believe this, but Roy is out of his coma, and he is talking to his mom and me. He is okay and so am I. I gave my heart to God. I am saved."

"That is wonderful news."

"I talked to his doctor, Dr. King; he is born-again too. Well, things had to happen to change me." "You are right, James, God does bring people to their knees. James, it is getting late I have got to hung this phone up. God bless you and your family"

"Same to you, Tom, see you soon. Okay, Tom, bye."

"Windy, do you know what happened? James got saved."

"Glory to God." said Windy. I knew it was going to happen. I know his wife must be happy. I know how I would feel if it were you, Tom. Sorry about your fishing trip."

"That is okay. God had it all planned out. He knows James was going to be saved. He still used you, Tom, to bring him in. Did you get to fish at all?"

"No. Windy, it happened when we were getting ready to fish."

"Tom, we have got a lot to thank God for."

"You are right, Windy. Just think, last week, if Jesus had come, James would have been lost. He is ready to go now. Thank God. We serve a good God."

"Yes, we do, Windy. He wants us all to go to heaven. He does not want any to perish. Windy how was your day?"

"So far, I guess okay. It is not that late. You have got to remember you all left early."

"Where is our daughter?"

"She is lying down in her room. Tom, I have some lunch, if you want to eat."

"Yes, that would be nice. Our sandwiches are still in the truck, and I have got to go get our car. We left it at James house. I think I will go and talk to Mary."

As Tom got to Mary's room, Mary was still in her bed but she was awake. She turned to see her dad.

"I heard what you told Mom, about Roy falling in the water. Is he okay, Day?"

"Yes, honey, he is, by the grace of God. I have some more good news."

"What, Dad?

"James got saved."

"Dad, that is good."

"Our Lord is so good. Would you like some lunch? I don't guess you have had breakfast, have you?"

"No, Dad, you all have not been gone too long. I went back to bed. I woke up when I heard you talking to Mom."

"What do you want? Your mom is getting something ready?"

"I will lie down after I have lunch."

"You all come on. I have lunch made."

"We are coming, Mom," said Mary.

"I am so tired I got up so early."

"You had better eat first," said his wife.

"I will," said Tom.

Everyone sat down. "Mom, it sure is wonderful that Mr. Johnson got saved."

"Yes, it is, Mary. But it is sad that his son almost lost his life."

"Now, Mom, he will go to heaven if anything happens."

The phone rang. "Mary, could you please get that?"

"Yes, Dad, I will. Hello, this is Mary Smith, who is this?"

"Mary, this is James Johnson . . . could I please speak to your dad?"

"Yes, Dad, it is for you."

"Who is it, Mary?"

"Mr. Johnson."

"Bring me the phone here," her dad said. "Hello, James, how is Roy?"

"He is better. Tom, the reason I called you, could you please bring my truck over to the house and my boat too?"

"I am home; sure I will be there in a little. Windy, I am taking James's truck and boat home. I will be back soon."

"Here is your coat. You will need it."

"I am sure, thanks, Windy. I will finish eating when I get back."

When Tom arrived at the Johnsons, he knocked at the door. Mrs. Johnson answered the door. "Hi, Mrs. Johnson, here is the keys to your husband's truck."

"Thank you, Mr. Smith."

"I have got to get back home. My wife had fixed us lunch. We were setting down to eat when your husband called me. Tell him I will talk to him later."

"Okay, Tom, you a have good day. Thanks again for bringing the truck home."

When Tom got home, his family had finished eating, and the kitchen had been cleaned up.

"Your food is in the oven when you want to eat it," said Windy

"Well, I will start supper later. You all just go in the living room, and we will have our Bible studies early." So that is what they did.

"Family, I want you all to know the rapture is going to happen soon. Luke chapters 17 to

26 tell you 'as it was in Noah days will be the return of Jesus.'

"Chapters 27 to 29, 'they did eat they drink they did married, they were given in marriage, until the day Noah went into the Ark, and the flood came, it destroyed them all, likewise also as it was in the days of Lot, they did drink the bought they sold they planted, they built but the same day that Lot went out of Sodom it rained fire from and brimstone from heaven, and destroyed them all, them all were even thus shall it be in the day when the son of man is revealed.'"

"Mom that is what is happening now?" said Mary.

"Yes, Mary it is. The Bible is already being fulfilled. We are waiting on Jesus."

"Mary, do you remember when Lot's wife looked back? She was turned into a pillar of salt."

"Yes, Mom, that is what the preacher said."

"Also, family, I have one more thing to add, in the day Jesus said 'in that day he witch shall be upon the housetop and this stuff in the house let him not come down Jesus said two will be in the field one will be taken one will be left, two women shall be grinding together the one shall be taken one shall be left.' So you see, Mary, not all will go; only the ones that loves Jesus.

"Yes, honey, you are right, but they all have a choice, for God or the devil."

"Now it is time for me to make supper, and then, we will go to bed. I am going to lead you all in a word of prayer, bow your heads. 'Dear Lord, we know it will not be long till you come take us home, we give you glory. Thank you, Lord, for healing Roy and saving James, help them to depend on you only. We give you glory, amen.'

"Now I will make some food; it is almost night time. We all will go to church tomorrow. Tom, you need to call James, see if they are going with us."

"Windy. I feel like they may want to be with their son. I will call. Here is the phone." James has dialed the number. "Hello, James, this is Tom."

"Yes, Tom, sorry I missed you. I was taking a shower after you left. My son called. We went to pick him up."

"Are you all going to church tomorrow?"

"Yes, we will see you there, okay? I will say good night."

"Good night, Tom, see you later."

Sometime during, the night, the rapture took place. It was morning time when over the TV, the news broke out.

"This is the channel 19 out of Georgia, we are getting breaking news. Many people are

disappearing off the earth. We have George Smith. Go ahead, George."

"Well, Tom, we are standing in front of the Western House School, and no one is here. It is after 10:00 a.m. Only a few teachers are here. Something happened; it is nothing like this before. We do not know what is going on. Well, Tom. I will give it back to you."

"Yes, thank you, George, there is lots of people calling in they go to look for their family."

They are gone. Wait, hello, yes lady, this is channel 19. My name is Tom Smith, can I help you? Calm down."

"My baby is gone. I cannot find her. What is going on?"

"Well, there are lots of people that are calling. I do not yet know. May be we will know later." People are calling. They cannot find their mother, dad, and children. One man called, he said the rapture had taken place. He was so upset. His name was John.

"What's wrong?" said the newsman. He began to tell him.

"My mom told me to get ready. Jesus was coming. I did not believe her. Now it has happened. I wish I had listened."

"What are you saying?"

"Well, my mom, she lived for the Lord, and she told us he was coming, we had better get ready."

"Maybe you have it wrong, John."

"No I didn't. My mom carried us all to church when we were little. She was at my house the other day, and now, this."

He hung up then the calls were nonstop. Terry, Mary's friend just woke up. She turned the TV on. She thought she was still asleep when she heard the news. Thousand have disappeared off the earth. This really brought back the time Mary had tried to talk to her about the rapture. Oh no, it has happened. She was so sad, she called Mary. She said to herself, maybe they were wrong.

She rang Mary's number. No answer. This really scared her. "Please, Lord, do not let this be true. I wanted so much to have you to come into my heart."

Terry felt so alone. "If only I had listened. Wait, I need to check and see if mom is here. I do not hear her moving around in her room. Maybe she is still asleep. No, Mom was ready to go. She gave her heart to God. I cannot fool myself, but I will go check. 'Mom, are in your room?' She could feel the tears falling down on her face. She did not want to face what she would see. She opened the door. No mom, only her clothes lying on the floor where she changed, her night gown in the bed. Terry lay her head on her on her mom's gown, crying. "I will call Dad," she said after she wiped the tears off her eyes. She rang the number. Her dad answered.

"Hello, Dad."

"Yes, Terry." He knew something was wrong. "Honey, are you okay?"

"Dad, I have been watching the news, lots of people are gone. What, Dad, are you talking about? Did you know about this?"

"Yes, honey, your grandma told me this. Honey, I will be at your house in a little. Where is your mom?"

"Dad, she is gone. She changed her life. I remember her telling me she was saved."

"Terry, why didn't you get saved?"

"Dad I do not know. My friend, Mary, talked to me, but it did not help."

"I am sorry. I am going over to Granny Jones. If she is gone, I will know the rapture took place,. I will be there soon."

"No, Dad, I am leaving now. I have got to know."

"Okay, I will be there when you get back. We need to talk."

Terry was talking to herself maybe granny Jones is there. "Then I will know everything is okay." On her way, she saw Mary's house. "I think I will check and see if Mary is home." But deep inside, she knew she was gone.

She went to Mary's house. She knocked on the door. No one come to the door. She began to cry. "Oh no," she said, "I wished I had listened to Mary. Now, I have got to go through the worst thing to come up on this earth."

Terry looked into the window but she saw nothing. It was so lonely in that house. "I wish I had got saved," she said to herself.

Terry left her friend's house still crying. She walked on to her granny. It seems so quiet nothing going on. She walked into the living room. "Granny, are you here? It is Terry, Granny."

No one answered. She walked into the bedroom. Granny's clothes and Bible were laid in her bed. It looked like she had just left.

She wanted to hurry and get home. The troubled truth had hit her in the face, but before she left, she kneeled down in her granny's bedroom to give her hear to God.

"Dear Lord. I am sorry for my sins. Please come into my heart and show me the way, right way, amen."

She was saved now, so if anything happens, she would go to heaven to be with her mom and granny, her friend Mary, along with her family. "If I had been saved, I would be in heaven now." She began to cry.

"I have got to stop this. I am almost home. Dad will be there. I will hurry." She began to run. The house looked so lonely. Her dad was sitting on the porch.

"Your granny was gone?"

"Yes, Dad. Dad what can we do?"

"Come let's go inside. I need for you to listen to a tape your grandma gave me. This is a long time ago. It is a tape that your grandma said her preacher gave to her to give to me. I went out one night when I was a young man. I got myself drunk. Mom was waiting up for me. I just knew she was going to get all over me, but she surprised me when she began to talk to me. She said, 'I am not going to bother you, because you know better. And if the good Lord comes tonight, you would be lost, and I want you to take this tape and watch it not only by you but others that might be left behind. This tape will tell you what to do. My preacher gave it to me for my lost love ones, and you are it.' You see, Terry, your grandma prayed for me. But just like you, I was young and thought I had plenty of time."

Terry's dad put the tape, it stated: "If you are watching this, you are left behind or you could be."

"Dad, I am so sorry. Grandma must have loved you so much."

"Yes honey, I would say so. Now listen to the preacher."

"The rapture has taken place. To the ones looking at this tape, you all have things to do. Please pray every day. God will help you to make the right move. He loves you so much, and you can still go to heaven. Please do not take the mark. If you do, your soul will be lost. You will have to be strong. Get with God's people. They are where you can find them. You all need to stick together, pray for each other. Jesus will be with you. He will has angels top watch over you."

"Terry do you have a fever?"

"What, Dad?"

"Well, your face is red."

"I am all right."

"Let me feel you. You are hot, Terry. Let's call your doctor."

"No, Dad I am not going to take the mark, Dad, I will die before I take it."

"Honey, let's call the doctor and see, okay? I have the number in my phone book. I will get it. Here it is."

"Dad, you can call."

The phone is ringing. "Hello, this is Dr. Johnson's office. My name is Judy Hill, may help you?"

"I am calling for my daughter, Terry Jones. She is sick."

"Sir has she been to this office before?"

"Yes, she has."

"Okay, let me find her record. Mr. Jones, can we see her at 2:00 pm today?"

"Yes, I will bring her."

"We have her set for 2:00 p.m. today. She will need to bring her ID card."

"Okay."

"How old is she?"

"She is ten years old. We will see you at 2:00 p.m."

"Terry you have an appointment with your doctor today at 2:00 p.m. today."

"So they are going to see me, Dad?"

"I guess so. You have to be there at 2:00 p.m. You need to get ready."

"Okay, Dad."

"I think I will make me a sandwich," said her dad.

"Dad, we do not have anything. Mom and I were going to get some groceries yesterday. But I did not have time. Today is Saturday. I am surprised they are open with what is going on. Things are different. We will see lots of thing that will surprise us. I will be out in a little. I do feel bad." "You will be okay in a little, Terry."

In a little, out walks Terry. "Let's go, Dad, I will lock the door."

"Dad, I miss Mom."

"I know you do, but one day we will see her again. Sometimes I miss her too. The time you were born, it was night time. Your mom got sick. It was raining real bad, lightning, and your mom is scared of lightning. So I had my job to get her to the hospital. So I covered her up and carried her to the car. You could not see her head, only her feet. Your mom was real small, so she did not weigh too much. After I got her to the car, I ran back to get her things and locked the door. We got to the hospital. She was happy to have you. You know, Terry, your name was picked before you were born."

"Dad, that makes me so sad. But one day, we will all be in heaven."

"Well, we are here let's go in. You sit there, I will talk to them."

"Okay, Dad."

"My daughter, Terry Jones, has appointment at 2:00 p.m. today. She is real hot. Is her doctor, Dr. Johnson, in?"

"Yes, he is, but I need to talk to you first. Did your daughter take the mark?"

"What are you saying?"

"Well, your money is no good. She will have to take the mark before the doctor will see her." "Dad I will not take the mark."

"No, honey, you will not. We will see if there is something at house for you we can pray."

"Dad, let's get out of here. Are you going by the grocer's store? If you do, you will get the same treatment that we got at the doctor's office."

"Terry, we will try and see what happens."

"It is not too far from here, Dad. We will have to lean on each other. You know, Dad, granny loves the Lord so much."

"Yes, Mom did. She would tell us stories about her childhood. She was raised in church too. Her dad, my grandpa, was real strict on his kids. There were things they had to do after school, and he made sure that they listen to him and grandma read the Bible. Well, here we are at the store. It doesn't look like too many in there. Let's go in. Well, you were right, look, Terry, they are paying with the mark.

"No, Dad, I will not do it. Let's go, it has happened. Dad, let's go home, it is getting late. We can find out on the TV what is going on. Dad, Granny told me that after the rapture, the mark of beast would come, and people will make a choice between heaven and hell. You know, Dad, people are so alone. They don't know what to do, what choice to make. But if they believe in God, it says then the kingdom of heaven be liked unto ten virgins which took their lamps and went forth to meet the bridegroom. Dad five of them were foolish, five were wise. The ones who were foolish carried their lamps and took no oil in their vessels. While the bridegroom tarried, they all slumbered and slept.

"And at midnight, there was a cry made, 'behold the bridegroom come go ye out to meet him,' then all the virgins arose and trimmed their lamps, and the foolish said unto the wise 'give us of your oil for our lamps have gone out, but the wise answer saying not so lest there be not enough for us, and you go to the one sold while they were gone the bridegroom come and the ones that were ready went in, they said Lord let us in, but he answer and said I know you not.' Dad that is like the rapture, some were ready and some were not."

"Well, let's watch the news now."

"Dad, there is the president."

"What is he saying?"

"Listen, Dad, can you believe what the president just said? He has gone crazy. He needs to be saved"

"Yes, honey, you right."

"Dad, do you want me to lead you in a sinner pray? It is very simple."Yes. Terry, I do."

The tears began to fall. "Dad, repeat after me. 'Dear Lord, I am a sinner. I need for you to forgive me. Come into my heart. I accept you as my Lord and savior. Thank you for the blood you shed for me. Help me to live for you so I can go to heaven, amen. Thank you, Lord.'

Now, Dad, you are forgiven of all your sins, and you are God's chosen child. He loves you so much."

"Yes, Terry, I feel so much better. Now we can see what the president is up to."

Newsman: "Mr. President, are you trying to tell us it is okay to take the mark?"

"Yes, Jim, that is what I am saying."

"Okay, so Mr. President, what makes you think that it is okay?"

"Well, sure that is the way I feel."

"Okay, Tom."

"Mr. President, what if the Christians are right, and the rapture has happened? What if you are wrong? You do believe in the Bible, don't you?"

"Well, there are lots of books written, don't mean they are true."

"Mr. President, are you saying the Bible is not true? And you do not believe in God? I believe in lots of things, but that does not mean they are real."

"Well that is our president, the one that has led our county. He sounds like he is in another world. He is saying nothing is true. Well, I can tell you one thing, lots of people are gone. Something happened to them; that is true."

"Terry, I am turning the TV off."

"Yes, Dad, it is bed time. You can sleep on morn's bed. We will see what happens tomorrow." "Terry, we need some answers. I will pray, see what God tells me."

"Me too, Dad. I will pray too."

"Good night, little girl"

"Good night, Dad. Sleep with Jesus."

"You too, he will never leave us." Terry began to pray, "Dear Lord, help us so we will know what to do. Lead us to others that know you, that believe in you, so we can pray together. Help my dad to put you first in his life. We need you more than ever, amen."

The night was different. Terry twisted and turned all night. She heard her dad in the kitchen. He was making coffee. "Well, Dad, I see you found the coffee."

"Yes, I did. Good morning."

Good morning, Dad. Did you sleep?

"Yes, I guess I was okay."

Terry turned the TV on. "Dad, the news is on. Some people are calling the newsroom. They do not want to take the mark. Some are trying to run away so they do not have to take the mark. Dad, let's get out of here. We do not want for them to find us here. We need to find Christian people and stay with them."

"Oka Terry, get ready."

"Dad, my face is not hot anymore. I was going to tell you about it when I got home, but now I just remember."

"I think God healed you. That is was I think," said her dad.

"He will heal us when we are sick. When we are need food, he will feed us like he did for the people in the days of Moses, led by God to promised land, he opened the sea to dry land." You are right, Terry."

"Dad, I am ready."

As they were going down the street, they saw people trying to hide themselves. The cars began to stop. A man came up to the car. "Can we help you? We are Christians. Come with us. We have a place for you all to stay."

Terry's dad did not have time to say anything before they were on their way to hide. They were still in their car, right behind the ones they were looking to find. They thanked God for his love in finding someone to help them. They stopped after they traveled some down a road they did not know.

You can park your car over there. No one will find us. God will help us to be okay. You all can go home to get what you need at night time."

As they entered the hiding place, they saw lots of God's people. A man named Chris began to talk welcome. He was a preacher. They had their families with them. Someone began to talk.

"My name is Tony. I need to speak to everyone. My family and me were left behind. I do not want to scare anyone, but we all need to pray that God will be with us. There are people out there that want to kill us, because we all believe in God. We will all stay here and help each other. When Jesus comes back, we will all go to heaven. I hope they do not find us. We will all pray. We cannot go out. The ones we brought here today, we will help them to get their things after it is dark."

"Dad, this is really bad. I wish I had been ready when Jesus came in the rapture, then I would be in heaven." Terry's dad stood up. "Do you all think anyone knows where we are at?"

"Yes, I guess they do," said Tony. "We are here because we are Christians. We can all lean on each other as God would want us to. Let's not be scared. Jesus is with us now."

At this very moment, an angel stepped forward. "You all are going to be okay. I was sent here from God to help every one of you, and no one can see me but you all that know God. Anytime you want to pray,

God is there. He will help every one of you all. I will stay as long as you need me. God loves you all so much. It may seem like you cannot make it. God has your back. He is with you now. You have nothing to worry about.

"Just because you were left behind does not mean you are alone. God sees you all. He knows you are so sad, and that you miss your love ones. Don't worry. You will see them again one day, as God would say, 'the one to the end shall be saved.' He is talking about you. You were left behind."

"I thank God. He is so good, Dad.

"It is getting night tune. We have got to get us some things from the house. Tony, we need to get our things from the house."

"Okay, you men lets help these folks get their things."

"Thank you all," said Terry.

"God bless you. Yes, we do," said her dad.

"Where do you all live?"

"It is off Howard street, not too far from here." "Our place is Highway 66 Street."

"I know where that is," said Tony.

"I do too," replied Sam. "We will watch while you all get your things."

"We do have a little food that we can bring with us."

"Okay, Dad, we can see what all we can come up with."

"You people watch what you are doing. I see a car light coming. It could be they are looking for us. It went on by. It must be someone else."

"Dad, here is a bag to put some things in. Here is some clothes you left here when you left Mom."

"Yes, you are right I did leave them here."

"Dad, here is some canned goods we can take with us." "Do you need anything else, Terry?"

"No. Dad, I have a few clothes in my bag. Dad let's not put our friends and us in danger." "I guess you are right, Terry, honey. I see your hair is so long like your mom's hair. It is so pretty. Your morn hair was black. Yours is like mine, brown. It is like God says your hair is your glory."

"Yes, Dad, I like my hair long. Well, Dad, let's go."

When they got to the car, Tony said, "Are you all ready?" "I think we should say a word of prayer, Tony."

"Yes, Mr. Jones, you are right. 'Father we are here because we did not follow you. We are sorry. Thank you, Lord, for our new friends. We need you to lead us your way, help us to understand what to do, and to put you first in our lives. We love you, Lord, amen."

"Dad, listen to what I read, 'Behold I stand at the door and knock.' Listen, Dad, it says 'if any men hears my voice and open the door, I will come in to and will sup with him and he with me.' Dad, the heaven is bright, with streets of gold. Dad it says in God's word there will be one hundred forty-four thousand people come out of the great tribulation and have washed their robes and made them white in the blood of the lamb. Dad this is while the tribulation is going on the fifth angel sounded and I saw a star fall from heaven unto the earth, and to him was given a key to the bottomless pit."

"Terry, honey, you are so young to know the Bible."

"Yes, Dad. But, Dad, if you have the faith of a mustard seed, you can do anything through God. "I guess you are right, Terry, go ahead and finish."

"And there came out of the smoke locusts upon the earth and unto them was given power as the scorpions of the earth have power and it was commanded them that they should not hurt the grass of the earth, neither any green grass."

"Dad, we will need God. This is what is going to happen before Jesus comes after us. It says there is going to be a bad time worse than ever before on this earth. No churches to go to, instead we have got to hide, and pray to our Father. He will help us, and we will be okay. God will tell us what to do if we will listen, that is all he asked. Dad, I will finish reading, okay?"

"Yes, go ahead."

"Neither any trees but only the men which have not the seal of God in their foreheads, and in them days shall men seek death. See, Dad, people are going to want to die. It is going to be so bad, and they shall not find it will flee from them (Matt. 24:21). And Dad, there shall be a great tribulation, such as was not since the beginning of the world to this time nor ever shall be shortened immediately after the tribulation of those days. Listen, Dad, the sun be darkened and the moon shall not give her light, and the stars shall fall from heaven, and the power of the heaven shall be shaken.

"Dad, just like the Bible said, it won't be long now until we go home to be with Jesus and our family. It says in God's word, there will be seven years tribulation, but with God 1000 years is counting as one day. I hope the ones that read my book, if they are not saved, give your heart to God. He is the only way. He gave his life for you. We are all sinners come short of the glory of God. All you have got to do is give your heart to God. Let Jesus come into your heart. He is the only way to heaven. If you are left behind, you have made the wrong decision. Please remember Jesus loves you."

Read your Bible. It will tell you what to do. I feel God wanted me to write this book, so it will help someone. Do not be like Terry and her dad and many more left behind. Make the right decision. Serve the Lord. Keep him in your life forever.

God so love the world he gave his only son that whoever believes in him shall not perish but have everlasting life (John, 3:16). Read it. You can go in the rapture. This is my story. Jesus is coming soon, be ready.

—Jeanie Breedwell

AUTHOR BIOGRAPHY

I was horn in the mountains of Alabama where we were farmers, had livestock, lots of rain, and snow. My school was miles away from our home, so I rode a bus. My daddy left me when I was three years old. My mom had eight children was the third from the last. My sister was older than me. She took care of me while Mom filled Daddy's shoes. I was a tomboy. I did whatever my brothers did. I moved to Florida in the 1960s.

BOOK 2

I am dedicating this book to Jesus Christ

When they got to the camp Terry said, "I am real scared, Dad."

"Terry, we will find some place to sleep. I have a gun. Do you think your dad needs it?" Terry's father replied.

"No, Dad, we need to depend on Jesus. He will watch out for us."

As they were talking, an angel appeared. "You are right, Terry. Your dad does not need a gun. Let God fight your battles. The people that are trying to kill you has the devil in them."

"You could talk to them; maybe they will change. Are you sure, Angel?"

"They may try to kill me, but they won't. They are made like you are. God made you all." The angel confidently said.

"Dad, I wish I could see my friend, Mary. She would tell me what to do."

"Honey, you will see her when we get to heaven. We must get some sleep now."

"Everyone else is asleep, Dad. I will do my praying now."

Terry got down on her knees, and prayed, "Dear Lord, my dad and I need your help. We do not know what to do. Please Lord keep us safe, let us be a witness for you. Help my dad to put his trust in you, only you. He did pray to you, asked you to come into his heart, I lead him in a sinner pray. I know Lord he loves you. Lord, help our friends to trust in you. Amen."

"Good night, Dad."

"Are you okay, Terry?"

"Yes, Dad. Why?"

"Because I know what you are sleeping on. It is hard, Terry. It will not be long before we will be with our Lord and Savior."

The next morning, Terry got up. She could smell the aroma coming from the kitchen. "Wow! That smells good."

"Dad, get up. I smell a nice breakfast cooking and coffee, too."

"Yes, you are right," said her dad. Terry and her dad entered the kitchen. They were stopped by one of the people living there, by one of the brothers.

"And we went uptown, saw some guys. They look like they were up to no good. I look for them to come after us. We need to stay hidden. We can trust in our Lord to help us to stand tall, not be afraid. If we do need to give our lives for the Lord, we can do it."

"He gave His life for us. These people won't leave us alone until we are dead."

"Dad, I am scared," Terry said.

"It is okay, Terry. Think of it this way: absent from the body is present with the Lord."

"Dad, I will try. I love my Jesus so much I could die for Him."

In came one of the sisters. "Tony, here they come."

"Oh, Dad, what do we do? They will torture us before they kill us."

"We will be okay, won't we, Dad?"

There was a strong voice that came from outside.

"All you so-called Christians come outside. You are going to take the mark. You do not want to be killed, do you?"

"Follow me, Terry."

"I am behind you, Dad."

You could see the tears coming from Terry's eyes as they made their way to the car.

They lined them up as they put them in the cars.

Terry still had tears in her eyes. She was holding on to her dad.

"Dad, this makes me wish I had been ready when the rapture came. We would be in heaven. Dad, I read the Bible and heaven is so beautiful and peaceful."

"Yes, Terry. Your grandmother read me the Bible, and she told me how big heaven was."

When they got to their stop, everyone got out.

Terry looked at her dad. One of the men said, "Which one wants to be first?"

"Dad, I will not take a mark. I will not betray my Lord. I will not take the mark. I would rather die than betray my Lord."

Her dad said, "I am waiting for someone to step forward."

"We are going to give you all a break. In the morning we will be back, then you all will take the mark. The ones that that give me trouble will answer to me."

"Dad, look there. Is that Angel?"

"Don't worry Terry, you will be okay. God is with you. Remember God's word where the king wanted Shadrach Meshach and Abed to bow down to their idols. 'We have our king we pray to, it is Jesus Christ,' they said. But the king said, 'You will bow to the idols, or I will throw you into the furnace. It will be real hot.' Shadrach Meshach and Abed replied, 'We do not care.' So the king did what he said. He looked in the furnace and he said, 'Did I not throw three men in there? I count four and one of them is the son of God.' So Terry, do not worry," said the angel. "God will be with you."

"Dad, I know God will never leave me or forsake me."

"I feel better, Terry, because what they do will happen in the morning.

"I do trust God. Dad, look, they have people line up to shoot them."

"Oh no, they are screaming. It's so bad. Look, Dad. Oh no, he cut off one of their heads."

"Terry, they are in heaven now. It's over for them."

The morning came early. Terry got up and called her dad. "Are you up, Dad?"

"Yes, Terry. I have been lying here thinking how we are going to stay alive."

"Me too, Dad. They will be here soon. They are going to kill us, Dad."

The Angel appeared once again. "You will be okay, Terry. God will help you to stay safe."

"Yes, Dad. He will."

"I see them coming." Terry began to cry. "Dad what will we do?"

"Okay, you so-called Christians. Come with me."

"Dad, I see a place that is open over there. Maybe we can run. Let's try." So that is what Terry and her dad did.

As they left, Terry said, "Where do we go from here?"

"Follow me," Terry's dad said, "let's try this road."

"Okay, I am with you, Dad. We will have to stay off the road. They will be looking for us."

"Look, Terry. Someone is in that ditch, hiding. Let's see if we can help."

"Wait," said Terry's dad, "we are Christians. Can we help you?"

"We were on our way to our hiding place," said the strangers, "We are also Christians. Come with us, we can hide you. My name is Paul. This is my family, my wife Judy, and our two boys, Ben and Larry. We are the Jacksons."

"We are the Joneses. This is my daughter, Terry, and my name is David."

"We were with some other people. It got so bad that we left. We found a way out. We were in our home when the rapture took place," said Mrs.

Jackson. "It was the reason we found out our baby girl was taken," the mother was crying.

"Don't cry, dear. You will see her one day."

"Yes, dear. You are right."

"I am so sorry, Mrs. Jackson," said Terry. "My mom was taken, and like you, I did not know for a while that it was the rapture. I turned on the TV and I heard something that took my breath away. I knew about it, but I thought I had plenty of time. Mary, my best friend, tried to get me to listen to her and change my life. I did not listen, I kept pulling it off. I thought it would be some time before it would happen. So you see, Mrs. Jackson, I was like you. I did not listen to my best friend.

All of Mary's family was ready to go, also the ones who lived across the road from them. Roy, their son, Steve, lead him in a sinner pray, then his mother, she got saved. And the dad."

"That is so good," said Mrs. Jackson. "My husband had been told that it would happen. This was by his own mother; but he never wanted to change. His sweet mother, the one that reminded him to pray. And the other kids passed away. Paul thought he had plenty of time. We did not think that our little angel, Rose, would be taken from us. I guess we did not stop to think it could happen."

"Wow. We have got to fight for our lives. Does your family know Jesus now that the rapture has happened?"

"Yes, we did. My family will go to heaven when Jesus comes back."

"That is good," said Terry, "You folks can stay with us. We can pray to God and He will keep us safe."

"Have you two ate anything?"

"No, Mrs. Jackson. That is okay. I think we can lie down and get a good night's sleep. My dad and I lived on Howard Street. We met up with other Christians and we stayed with them until we got caught, then we made our way out the back way. We have been looking for someone to help us. Then we found you all. We feel God sent our way. I wish I had listened to my friend Mary. She was my best friend, every time I was with her, she would witness to me."

„Granny Stone, I miss her so much."

"I am sure you do, Becky. But you will see her again."

"She would not miss going to church and you know, Terry, she drove us there. And she was old."

"What about your mom and dad?"

"I do not know. I looked for them. I could not find them. I have been living with Granny Stone for a long time. She was so good to me. She bought my computer. I really like it."

"Did you ask her for it?"

"Yes, I did."

"On my way here, I saw some of them bad people. I ran into the old house down the road. It was empty."

"Becky, are you saved?"

"No."

"Would you like to be?"

"Yes, I would."

"Okay, repeat after me. Dear Jesus, I know I am a sinner. I ask you to forgive me of my sins. Come into my heart. Amen."

"Now you are a Christian, Becky. You will go to heaven."

"Thank you, Terry."

"You are welcome. Jesus loves you so much, He wants you to live for him."

"Terry, it will be okay with God's help. We can pray for each other."

"Thank you, Mrs. Jackson."

"You are so welcome. Did I hear someone at the door?"

"I do not know," said Terry. "Let me check."

Everyone tried to hide until they heard a soft voice, "Anyone there?"

"Yes," said Mrs. Jackson.

"Who is it?" Mrs. Jackson opened the door. "Come on in."

"Can I stay with you all?"

"Sure," said Mrs. Jackson.

"What is your name? Are you alone?"

"My name is Becky, Mrs. Jackson."

"Yes, Terry. Becky is a friend of Mary. You know I told you about Mary.

"Hi, Becky. Mary spoke of you many times. You went to her church. Your Grandma and you.

That is right," replied Becky.

"What happened?"

"Well, I was left behind."

"I thought I was saved. My Grandma told me about Jesus."

"Where do you live?"

"I live on Jay Street with my Grandma. I got up the day the rapture happened. She was gone.

"Mary talked to you about getting saved?" "Yes, Becky. Many times."

"Why did you not listen to her?"

"I do not know. I cannot say. She told me about the rapture and that it would soon happen. I thought I had plenty of time. Now she is gone, she is with Jesus."

"Becky, do you want anything to eat?"

"Yes."

"We do have some hot dogs and there is some Coke. It is hot, but it is something to drink, said Mrs. Jackson.

"That is okay. I ate a little at Granny. She had some things that was okay to eat."

"Okay, girls, we need to get some rest. Becky can sleep with you Terry, said Mrs. Jackson.

When Terry and Becky got into the room, Terry said, "Becky. One thing we do as Christians is that we pray. Pray with me, Becky. Dear Jesus, be with us tonight and all our friends. Keep us in your loving arms until you come and take us home."

Mrs. Jackson came to the door "Sorry girls, but we have no lights, I will not take the mark.

"We will ask God to be with us."

"Yes, it is dark."

"Here is some candles for you girls. But put them out before you go to sleep."

"We will, Mrs. Jackson."

"Dad."

"Yes, Terry. I am thinking about what happen when the rapture occurred. I saw cars on the highway. Some of them went out of control and ran into other cars. I saw a blue car. It's moving fast all at once. It lost control and ran off the highway. It threw people out of the car. A plane fell out of the sky, it hit the ground and it exploded. My, what a loud noise."

"Terry, she could hear people crying. They were trying to find their families. They were screaming so loud. All the lights were out in the homes. Terry could see so much she was scared."

"Dad, I just saw the rapture happen."

"What are you talking about Terry?"

"I saw people all over the highway. And they were dead."

"Terry you need to go to bed. Maybe things will be different tomorrow."

"We need to keep each other in our prayers. Good night, Dad."

"Good night, Terry."

And Becky said, "Good night, sir. See you all in the morning."

"When Terry got back in bed, she asked Becky, "Are you going to try and find your parents?"

"I do not know, Terry. I would not know where to look for them."

"I can help you."

"Thank you, Terry."

"Do you think your mom and dad made it in the rapture?"

I do not think they made it the way I remember things. They did but they could have."

"I sure hope so. I have not seen them in a while."

"Where do they live?"

"Where I was raised. They have lived there for awhile."

"Do you know where that is at Terry?"

"Yes, my dad lived on Howard. That is where my mom and I lived before the rapture. My mom was ready to go; I wish I had been."

Terry said, "Becky, I am going to sleep. See you in the morning."

"Okay. Good night, Terry."

The next morning the two girls got up. "Dad how did you sleep?"

"Okay, I guess."

"I pray for Jesus to take care of us. Folks, I would offer you some food but my boys ate it all."

"There is some cold coffee."

"That is okay," said Terry.

"Yes," said her dad. "They need it more than us."

"Me, too," said Mrs. Jackson.

"I do not know what we will do without food."

"We will make it," said Terry's clad. "God will see to it that we have food. Remember when Moses led the children to the Promised Land, they were not to worry because God led them manna from heaven, day by day, hey had plenty to eat."

"You are right." said Terry. "God will make sure we have fwd. He will give us water and food, keep us safe from harm. Many times He put things in the path of the enemy so they could not hurt God's people. We are not supposed to worry about anything. We put our trust in God."

"Yes, Dad. I will pray every day."

"Mrs. Jackson called out to Terry." Yes. Could I get everyone to come to the kitchen?

"We will be right there."

"I have something to tell everyone."

"We are here."

"There is a house up the road. We need to find a place to hide. We can go to that house I told you about. We need to leave now."

"You boys get your coats and I will get us some cover. Dad, we can get some things. It will give us something to lie on."

Mr. Jackson stepped outside, then he came back in. "We can leave now. I do not see anyone."

"We can leave out the back door." All the people started to leave.

"It is not too far from here. And that is where we will be going."

"We can walk over to the side of the road."

They were all walking behind each other.

"Dad, when we get there, I pray we can eat."

"Dad, we are here."

"Wait, someone is here."

"You people Christians?"

"Yes, we are."

Tony said, "You all come on in."

"Thank you," said Mrs. Jackson.

"We have got to watch who we let in our borne," said Mr. Owens. "This is my wife Peggy and my name is Ray. We are the Owens. We have been here for a while. We have been watching. We do not trust anyone. We have our guns and we gave our hearts to God after the rapture so we will not use our guns. We will trust in God to take care of us. Are you hungry? We do have some food if you all would like to eat."

"Yes, thank you," said Terry. "I could eat a little, and I am sure the rest of our group could eat. It is real nice of you all to help us."

"We do not mind."

"Yes." said Mrs. Jackson. "We were in our home when we heard someone outside. Terry, her dad, David Jones, and Terry's friend. Becky.

We were doing okay until we all felt like we need to move to a safe place."

"You all are welcome here," said Mrs. Owens. "We can all pray for each other that God will keep us under His wing. We have some beds where our children sleep when they live here with us. They were all saved. Our daughter, Cathy, she was a pastor. She tried to get her daddy and me to change. But Ray and I thought we had plenty of time. I hear my daughter at night time praying for her dad and me to get saved. She loved the Lord so much. She had been married, but her husband tot killed at the store he worked at. She did not look at another man. She let God lead her. You could see it in her eyes."

"I guess you all know we will be without lights and water because I will not take the mark of beast."

"Everyone, it is getting late. We all need to get some sleep."

"Mr. Stone, would you please lead us in a word of prayer?" said Mrs. Owens.

"Sure, I will. Let's all join hands. Keep our mind on Jesus. Dear Lord, we want to thank you so much for the blood you shed for us all. Thank you, Lord, for leading us to these nice people. Help us, Lord, to stand up for you. Help us to lead the lost souls to you. We love you, dear Lord. Amen."

"Okay, Terry honey, you can sleep in Cathy's room. I will show you where it is."

"Wow, it's real pretty."

"Yes. Cathy did keep her room clean."

"I see her Bible on her bed."

"I will move things around for you."

"I can do it."

"Terry, my sweet Cathy was real small. So if you want to wear her clothes, you and Becky can. I know she would not mind. Here is a couple of night clothes for you and your friend. Becky can sleep with you."

"Becky, come here."

"I am coming, Terry."

"Okay. What do you want? You can sleep with me in Cathy's bed. It is real big. And here are some sleeping clothes for you. Mrs. Owens said we could have them."

"Yes, Becky that is true."

Mrs. Owens went back into the kitchen.

"Mr. Stone."

"Yes, can I help you?"

"I just wanted you to know your daughter and her friend are sleeping in my Cathy's bed. Mr. and Mrs. Jackson, you both can sleep in the next room."

"Mr. Stone, you will sleep in the room next to your daughter. The boys I will make a bed on the couch."

The next morning someone was knocking on the door. Mrs. Owens went to the door.

"This is the light man. You will need to pay your lights. You are behind."

"Mrs. Owens, they will not take money."

"You will have to take the mark."

"I will not take no mark."

"Hold on, Mrs. Owens. I will be back."

The light man called his boss. "Bob, this is Tommy. Yes, I am at the Owens. She owes a bill. I told her she would have to pay with a mark. She told me no. What do I do?"

"You will have to turn them off."

"That is bad, Bob."

"We cannot help it. That is the way it is."

"Okay. Thanks. See you later."

"Mrs. Owens, I will have to turn off your lights." He showed her what three numbers she would need.

"Not me. I will not take it. You can turn them off."

"I will not pay that way at all. I read my Bible and it says if you take the mark, you will go to hell. I love my Lord too much."

"Okay, Mrs. Owens. Sorry."

Mrs. Owens went inside.

Everyone was up.

"What has happened?"

"That was our lights. They are turned them off because I will not take mark of beast."

"My dad and I will not take the mark. We are going to heaven."

"We are, too," said Mrs. Jackson.

Terry was watching out the window. "You guys, there is a car outside. They are getting out."

A woman and a man came out.

"Becky, is that your mom and dad?"

"Yes, it is."

Becky ran to the door. Becky's mom and dad said, "We were looking for you. We hope you had gone with your grandma. We knew she was okay and she would go in the rapture."

"Yes, Mom. I have been praying for you and Dad."

"Yes. I wish we had listened to your Grandma Stone. She went to the Church every time the doors open."

"Yes. Mom. I hear her pray many times for us to be saved and go in the rapture. She did talk to me and told me Jesus is coming."

"Come on in, Mom and Dad. This is Terry, her dad, Mr. Jones."

"Terry, this is my mom and dad. We are the Stones. Dad, Mom, this is Mr. and Mrs. Owens, they are the Jackson, and their two boys, Larry and Jeff."

Becky asked, "Where were you and Dad at?"

Mrs. Stone replied, "We were at our house. When it was not safe, we went out the back door to come here. We thought it was empty."

"Mom, we can stay together. I miss you and Dad so much. My friend, Terry led me in a sinner prayer. I gave my heart to Jesus."

"That is good, Becky. Your dad and I gave our hearts to God, too. We were so foolish when we did not listen to what your grandmother said. We could have went in the rapture."

"It is time to eat. We do have a few eggs and bread left if anyone is hungry," said Mrs. Owens. "It is on the table, Mr. and Mrs. Stone. You all can stay with us."

"We will help each other. We have some food in our car. Dear, could you get it for us?" said Becky's mom.

"Sure, I will get it now."

"Becky you want to help your dad?"

"Yes, Dad, I will."

Everyone went into the kitchen.

"I will just find you a place," said Mrs. Owens. "We all need to do what we can before dark. We have no lights."

"Mom, they turned off these good people's lights," said Becky, "just this morning.

"Because she would not take the mark."

"Yes, that is right. We will all be okay. God is with us."

"Mom, I feel hot," said Larry.

"What is wrong son?"

"I do not know."

"Why don't you lie down, son. I will get something for you. I think I have some Tylenol on my dresser."

"Is he okay," said Mrs. Owens.

"Yes, he will be okay. He has been sick for awhile. We can pray for him."

"Yes, Mrs. Jackson said.

"Terry, I was sick right after the rapture, and God healed me. My dad carried me to the doctor's. They wanted me to take the mark. I told Dad no, so we left the doctor's office. I was burning up, my face was real hot. But that night, the fever broke. I told Dad later I felt better. I never took anything."

"Let's pray for Larry."

"Yes, we can," said Terry's dad.

"Larry, do you want us to pray for you?"

"Yes, mom. I do not feel good at all."

"Brother Stone, could you pray for my son?"

"Yes, sure. Let's all hold hands around Larry. We are blocking the enemy. The blood of Jesus is here with Larry. Dear Jesus, You said in Your word that wherever there are two or three gathering In Your name You would be there. You have got to go, devil. Take your hands off Larry. In the sweet name of Jesus, we claim his healing now. Thank you, Lord, for all you are doing for your people. Now is the time we call out to You until You come for us. Amen. Everyone let's let Larry rest.

He is going to be okay."

"I feel it," said his mom. "Let's all go to the living room. Mrs. Owens, is it okay for Becky and I to go to Cathy's room? I feel at peace in there."

"Sure. You both can light your candle. She has some dolls you both can play with."

"Dad, we will be in Cathy's room if you need me."

"Okay, dear. I will sit here and rest."

"Okay, Dad."

"Terry, your dad wants to walk for a while and see what is going on. Would you go with me, Paul?"

"Yes, I would like that. I need to walk for a while."

As they were going down the road, David said, "Look, Paul, all the lights are out."

"Yes, David, I see. That's sad for some folks. If they do not have God to help them, they may take the mark. We will have to hide until we find a safe place to stay."

"Paul, let's go back because we do not have a light to see. With all the things going on, it could be bad."

"You know, Paul, I do not know what is going to happen. My mom gave me a Bible but I did not read it."

"Yes, David. I know what you are talking about. My mom, they called her one of the praying women of Georgia. She kept her mind on God. She loved everyone. We all were going to Church from the day we were born. My mom prayed for us all the time. She had her hands full with us kids, and there were eight of us."

"Yes," said David, "My mom made sure I went to church. I was the only child. She loved me so much. When I was a young boy I went out one night, got drunk, and I thought my mom was going to whip me.

But she did not. She talked to me and she gave me the worse time of my life. She felt bad. I know she did."

"You would think with the teaching my mom did, I would be ready to go. My daughter, Terry, had a real good friend. Her name was Mary, and she talked to Terry all the time about the rapture. Not one day that she did not remind my sweet daughter to get ready. My Terry was not thinking about her soul. She did not listen. I wish she had. Them people were one of a kind. They were out to get people saved."

The little boy across the street Steve talk to him. His name was Roy,

Steve lead Roy in a sinner pray. Steve mom visit Mrs. Johnson to make friends.

When they talk Steve mom found out Mrs. Johnson got saved.

Witch made Steve mom happy, then Mr. Johnson got saved because he almost.

Lost his son Roy, that is what the Smith.

Wanted to accomplish to get as many saved as they could,

"They knew that the Johnson were ready for the rapture.

"You were saying your daughter, Terry, should have got saved?"

"You know, David, my wife and I were doing things we almost lost our home, our lives were upside-down. We left our boys, Jeff and our youngest Larry alone just so we could drink and be with our friends. We went to bars and thought we were having a good time. We were not looking for Jesus. We knew it was going to happen, but we did not think of the rapture. We thought it would happen at the tribulation time. It was a surprise to Judy and me after we heard it on the news. We got down on our knees and gave our heart to God. The boys, too. We had them to do the same."

"Sorry, Paul. My daughter Terry called me, she was so upset. She thought it was a dream. It happened at night time. Her mom was ready to go, I think. Terry's friend, Mary, had something to do with that because just before the rapture, Mary went shopping with them. She was trying to get Terry to give her heart to God. My daughter did not listen. Terry's mom asked what her and Mary what they were talking about. Terry told her mom they were talking about Jesus and they started talking about going to Mary's church. At her church, they don't preach of the rapture. Terry called me and said her mom had changed. So God took Terry's mom in the rapture. One day we will all be together."

"Paul here comes a car. Let's get out of here. They are everywhere. We will have to hide."

They were back at the house. Terry answered the door.

"Dad, where were you? I started to worry. You were gone for a while."

"Terry, remember I told you I was going for a walk, Paul and me? All the houses around here are without lights. I guess when they turn these lights off, everyone else's was turned off."

"They did. I saw him do it, the light man," said Mrs. Owens. "I guess so," said Terry.

"It is so lonely around here since our loved ones are gone," said Mr. Owens.

"Yes, it is. I know. I miss my Cathy. She was so good and she loved the Lord. He is who she lived for."

"Mrs. Jackson, how is Larry?"

"He is doing good. I checked on him a few minutes ago. He is still asleep. When you all get ready to go to bed, you can sleep in the same bed you did last night. We do not have any more food."

"We will depend on the Lord."

The next morning came early. Mrs. Owens went outside. She got the morning paper.

"I read in the paper that there is going to be a meeting at the court house. The president and the Anti-Christ will be there. They will be speaking. He said that they were going to give us good news."

"I do not believe that," said Mrs. Jackson.

"It's a trick. He wants to get us all together so he can kill us. I will not take the mark. I will not give him the privilege to put a devil's mark on me. God will take care of us."

"Paul, let's go to this meeting. Let's try to slip in to the people and see what is going on. We can hide; they will be so many and they will not see us."

"Mrs. Owens, what time will it start?"

"It says the president will be speaking at 4:00 p.m." "Okay, we have plenty of time."

"Dad, do you think you will be okay?" said Terry.

"Sure, honey. I will be okay. I want to see what is going on in this world."

"Okay, Dad. I will pray for you."

"Mr. Stone, here is one of my husband's coats. Here's one for you, Mr. Jackson. It may be a little big. But it will serve the purpose. My husband is a big man."

"Yes, dear I am. I do have a few years on them."

"You do, dear Paul. I will pray for you and Mr. Stone. Are you sure this is what you both want?"

"It is dangerous. Yes, it is. But we have a merciful God to lead the way."

Mr. Stone went outside. He looked to the side of the house then he saw the Angel, the same one that he and Terry saw the day they found the Christian people.

"You, I have seen you before."

"Yes, you are right. Only God's people can see me. You are okay."

"Me and Brother Paul are going to the meeting."

"Yes, you all need to know what they are planning on doing. I will go with you."

"Okay, Angel. Thanks."

The time is passing by it is near 4 p.m.

"Paul, we need to get ready."

"Yes, David I will hurry."

"We still have our water, but we had better do what we can to get ready."

"They will turn it off, too," said Mrs. Owens.

"Paul, I saw an angel outside when I went outside early."

"It was the same one my daughter and I saw after the rapture. He will be going with us."

"God's people is the only one to see him."

"That is good," said Paul.

"Let's finish getting ready. I will get a bath first."

"Okay, Paul. We need to get on the road."

"Dad, I will stay with Mrs. Owens. Becky and I. we will stay in Cathy's room. I will play with Cathy's things. They are real pretty."

After Paul took his bath, he said, "Are you ready, David?"

"Yes, I am."

"We will be praying for you both, said Mrs. Owens.

"Thank you. We will need God's help. We will need to make good judgment.

As they were leaving, Paul gave his wife a kiss.

"Bye. See you all when we get back."

When David and Paul got up the road. David asked, "Do you know where it is?"

"We take this road to west to 63rd Street and make a left, then go to the red light and make a left. It will be on the right at Washington Street."

"Okay, here we go. Angel are you here?"

"Yes, I am."

"This is Paul, my friend."

"I know."

"Oh, I forgot you know everything."

"Yes, I do."

"Glad you are here."

"You both will be okay," said the angel.

"We are here, David."

"Yes. There are lots of cars here. People gathered around the court house. We will not be able to get too close. There are lots of people here."

"Look, David. There is the president, and another man wearing black.

They are getting ready to speak.

The president first. He said, "Hello, everyone. Welcome to our meeting. I know without a doubt we can make things better. How many here have lights?"

Paul looked at all them with their hands raised.

David said, "They are the ones that took the mark. Sad to say, but they cannot be forgiven for they have sold their souls to the devil."

"Yes, David, you are right."

The president again said, "Now don't it feel good to have lights? You can have food. You can have TV. Your kids will be happy. They can do what they want, too."

David said, "I will not sell my soul to hell."

"David, I am with you," said Paul.

The president said, "It is okay to take the mark. Nothing will happen to you. You will be okay. You will get everything free. All you have got to do is show the number."

"This makes me sick," said David.

"Me, too." said Paul.

The president continued speaking, "So the ones, who want the number, come here tomorrow between 3 and 4 p.m. and we will meet here at the court house and then you will have it done that same day. If your lights are off, they will turn them back on."

"Mr. President, do you not know that the mark will send you to hell?"

"Bill that is an old saying from them crazy Christians. They do not know."

"Mr. President, question: where do you think all the people went when they disappeared? This was a few nights ago."

"What are you saying, Tom? Look at what is here. It does not look like anyone is gone."

"But Georgia is such a small place. There are people gone."

"Look around you. Look at the tears in the ones that have missing family."

"Well, I do not know. But look at what we can do for the ones left behind. They will not have to do without if they will take the mark. They do not need money,

just a number that you can show. See, Tom, we have the answer for the people's problems."

"What can you do, Mr. President?"

"What about you, Tom?"

"I just write the news. You are the one to take care of the USA, not me"

"That is what I will do if they will listen to me."

"I hope they do not listen to you. Mr. President."

"Wait one minute, Tom. You will have to take the mark to tell the news."

"What are you saying, Mr. President? I will not take a mark for you or anybody."

"Tom, our conversation is over."

"Fine with me."

"Hold on, Tom. You guys grab him. He will go to jail now."

"Look. Paul. What they are doing to that newsman."

"You cannot do this, " said Tom, the newsman. "Let go of me."

One of the men that had Toni hit him in the head. Tom had blood running down his face. They put Tom in a black car and took him away.

"Now that he is gone, we will finish. He is the news now. I want everyone to meet the man that made this possible and he will make your dreams come true."

"Everyone let me give you the ones that made it possible. People of Georgia, hello."

"Hello."

"Everyone, how many would like to live the life of luxury? Have anything you want, make your child happy with the things you will get. The sky is the limit and without a hassle. You women can have anything you want. No money; you only show the mark. It will not hurt you. I promise. You will go to store and get what you want. Oh yes, you can have your drugs if you want to get high. There is nothing that you cannot get. You men can wear nice clothes; paints that cost nothing. Just show the number. Ladies, how about a nice dress that cost nothing?

Eat steak every day, have the best car to drive, and a boat to go fishing."

"You guys, your children can have all the toys you want."

That is nice.

"Have your own phone."

"Look, Paul, how he is trying to get next to the kids, then he will be able to get to the mom and dad. Watch him hold that baby and smile. I know what he is up to. He is playing on the ones that are poor. Look at the people over there. They have never had everything. Them is the ones he will talk to."

"Everything is going to be fine, you have me to help you, and I will. This is goes for the ones who will take the mark only. The others will not get anything, they will only depend on their God. They will get nothing from me; I owned it all. The ones who take the mark will live in the nice home. Ladies, anything you want to wear, and jewelry, any kind you want. We will take the names of the ones who want to have anything their hearts desire."

"Listen, Paul, to that. They will sell their soul to the devil. And once it is done, they cannot change their mind. See what is happening. Paul? Everyone that is close to us have taken the mark."

"It is so sad. This devil worshipper has everyone in his hands. Let's go before they see us."

"Hold on, Paul. Let's see what they say.

"For the ones that do not take the mark will be killed," the president said.

"Watch. He has the mark. He is showing it now to the crowd. He is crazy, I think. They do not know what they are doing. Remember when Jesus gave His life for us? He told the Father to forgive them because they did not know what they were doing. He knew the devil had them in his web."

"See? My family is happy. Nothing will happen to you if you take it.

Someone in the crowd said, "Look. I do not mind, Mr. President. I will have what I want. My mom and dad have been poor all their lives. Now we can get nice things. I want me a motorcycle and I can pick out what color I want."

"Right," Mr. president said, "Yes, that is right. Anything you want if you will take the mark."

"What mark?"

"You do not understand? There is not going to be any money."

"You will have to show the number. How old are you? I am 16 years old."

"Oh, no. Mom what is he talking about? My grandmother told me if you take the mark you will go to hell. I did not understand I do not want to go to hell. My grandmother, where did she go, Mom?"

"Honey, she was ready to go in the rapture."

"Junior," his mom whispered, "you do not have to take the mark.

"But mom, grandmother told me that they will kill you."

A young girl named Judy stepped forward. "Mr. President, I want me a car."

"Judy, all you have got to do is take the mark."

"See, I have it. I wish you all would take the mark. Then you can live like kings and queens."

"How does that sound?"

"Another step forward, but when you take it, you go to hell."

"No, young man. Where did you hear that?"

When we were going to church, the preacher said it. If you take the mark you will be selling your soul to hell."

"No, that is hogwash," said the president. "No truth to it. You will be okay if you take the mark. You will be happy you will see."

Another newsman asked, "Mr. President, where do you think the people went that no one have found babies?"

"Mr. President, do you not believe in God?"

"Well, I guess so. What do you believe about God? There are many gods. People have their own gods that they pray to."

"So you have your own?"

"I know what I can do for the people if they will let me."

"If you want a doctor, there is one for you. Food you can get with your number. Why would you not like that?"

"Just to be rich not with money, but with a number. Mr. President, are you telling me to take the mark? And you say I want go to hell?

That is what you are saying, Yes that is what I am telling you. Now I will turn it over to the father o times.

Christ everyone that takes the mark if you need anything.

You will get it from me,

I have everything under control it all belongs to me, I take the seat o your God.

You will worship me now I am the beast.

But there is love for the ones that bow down and worship me if you need anything.

I have it listen Paul that is in the Bible it is what God.

Said would happen.

"Paul, let's go I have had enough of this. It makes me sick. They control everyone and they are like starving pigs to believe what they told them. How do we get out of this place without bringing attention to ourselves?"

"We will go this way. It is dark. Hold on, I brought a flashlight. I wonder what time it is now."

"It was good you brought it, Paul. Now we can see our way home."

"David, we will have to be quiet when we get to the house. Everyone will be in bed without lights. It will be dark. Here we are. I will open the door. Mrs. Owens gave me a key to get in.

"It is us," said Paul. Terry came running.

"Dad, you had me so scared."

"We are okay. We will tell everyone what we found out tomorrow. You will not believe it."

The night was so long. Terry keep her dad awake most of the night.

"Dad, it is getting so bad down here. I miss my best friend and my mom. There is not a day goes by that I do not think of them both."

"Honey, I will pray that God keeps His hands on us all."

"Dad, it seems as we are going to hide all the time from them people. They want to control us. They have the devil in them."

The next day, Terry ran to her dad. "Let's go to the kitchen."

"Yes, I will get some coffee."

"Paul, you tell them what we found out. I have got to calm my daughter down.

She was so scared."

"Dad, I am okay now. Everyone, gather around Paul and me. We will tell you what we found out."

"Paul, you go first."

"We found out there is going to be a meeting again today. The ones who want the mark will get it. The president had them all believe that they will be okay to take the mark, and they can get anything they want without money."

"Dad, we are not going to take it, are we?"

"No, honey. It is time to eat. Terry, we will not sell our soul to the devil. I did have a few canned goods in the room for them who wants anything. Here are some canned goods. It is cold but it is better than nothing. Look, here is some bread."

"That looks good."

"But it cannot be, unless God put it there.

"The angel stepped forward.

"Yes, you are right," said the angel.

"God did put it there."

"Who are you?" said Mrs. Owens.

"David let me be the one to tell you who he is. He is an angel from God.

He came to us after the rapture."

"What?" said Mrs. Jackson.

"Yes, that is right," said Terry. "He came to us now. We know who is saved if you see him."

"Mrs. Jackson, you see the angel. The only way you can see him is if you are saved. He went with Paul and David to hear what the president had to say."

"I can talk," said the angel.

"It was not so good. The president knows he can get the poor people to take the mark. You see children, the ones that are saved, will not take the mark because they trust in our father, God. And they will be okay until our Father God comes back. Now please eat what our Father God has for you. Remember, God wants you to know that absent from the body is present with the Lord. You all pray for each other. That is all you need to do. He knows what you are going through."

There is a knock at the door.

"Let the stranger in. They are looking for you all."

"Come on in."

"We are looking for the Christian people."

"We are all here," said David.

"Yes. You all come on in. My name is Judy, this is my husband Ray. We are the Evans. And this is Jeanie and her husband Kenny, and my daughter, Sally. We are all saved but my daughter Sally. We are the Johnsons. We live next to each other."

Terry stepped forward. "Hi, my name is Terry. Come with me to my room, where we stay. This is my friend Becky. We are all saved. Sally, would you like to be saved?"

"Yes," said Sally.

"Thank God. Let's go be with my dad and the rest so we can all pray."

"Dad, this is Sally. Sally, this is my dad."

"Mr. Stone, pleased to meet you."

"Same here, said Sally."

"Dad, Sally wants to be saved."

"Good. Terry will you all pray with us? Honey you know how to lead Sally in a sinner's prayer."

"Yes, Dad, I can. But can't we all pray together?"

"Sure. Listen everyone, we have a young lady here that wants to be saved. Let's all hold hands and we will pray for Sally."

"Okay, Terry. You have the floor. Lead your new friend in a sinner's prayer."

"Okay, Dad. Sally repeat after me. Dear Lord, I come to you a sinner. I ask you to forgive me of my sins. I want to serve you and stand up for you when the devil comes around me. As my stay on earth until you come again for me to take me to heaven. I love you, Lord. Amen. Now, Sally. Welcome to the kingdom of God.

You will go to heaven now. You are the child of God. He loves you so much. It is time to eat what God has for us."

"Thank you, Terry," said Sally, "I feel better."

Sally hugs everyone.

"God be with you," said the children of God.

"Mr. and Mrs. Johnson and Mr. and Mrs. Evans, would you like something to eat?

We just got, through God, bread, and I had some canned goods I put up last year. You all are welcome to it."

"You people are real nice. Come with me," said Mrs. Owens, "You can sit here,

Mrs. Johnson."

"Do you think your little girl would like something?"

"I will see."

"Sally."

"Yes, Mother?"

"Would you like something to eat?"

"Yes. Mom."

"Come here. I will make you a plate. Here is your plate."

"I need to have everyone to come to the kitchen," said Mrs. Owens. "We have got to leave from here. It is going to get rough, we need to keep moving."

"Yes," said Paul. "You are right."

"What the president said, we are on quick sand. It is bad. But God will help us."

"Dad, I will get my things so we can move from here. We all can stay together. That is what God would want us to do."

"Is everyone ready? We will leave out the back door."

"There is a place that Paul and I saw as we were going to the court house," said David.

"Dad, I am so scared."

"It's okay, little girl. We will pray that God will be with us."

"Dad, what will we do?"

"Honey, you follow your dad."

"Okay, Dad. I am so glad Sally got saved. Now she will go to heaven."

"Yes, Terry, She will. The rest are behind us."

"Dad, I miss mom. I wish I had listened to Mary. She is happy now. Dad, do you think Mary knows I did not make it in the rapture?"

"I do not know, Terry."

"I do not think she does. It would make her sad. God would not allow that."

"Everyone there is a place just a few miles ahead of us. We can stay there tonight. Then we will move on at night time."

"Dad, look at the bright star. God has given us light."

"You are right, Terry. Let's all bow down and thank God."

"Yes, we can do that. David, would you lead us in a word of prayer?"

"Yes, I would love to. Lord we feel like the men in the fields the time you were born when you put a star in the sky so they could follow it to your birth. Thank you, Lord, for that. We know you are ahead of us so we will not fall. No darkness will be in our way. The light will take us where will be safe, and we will give you the glory, and all God's people will say 'Amen."

"Okay, everyone, we are almost there."

"Yes," said Mrs. Johnson.

"I know where that is. No one has lived there in a while. The women who owned it passed away, so I am sure it has everything we need."

They have arrived at the house.

"Look, Dad, a swing. I will sit on it."

"No, honey, we all need to go inside."

"Paul, do you still have your flashlight?"

"Yes, David, I do."

"We need it now. Let Paul go first."

Paul was moving the light around checking it out.

"Look, Dad, a Bible."

"Yes, Terry. These folks were ready to go. They have food here."

"I do not understand," said Mrs. Johnson. "No one has lived here in a while."

"Well, Mrs. Johnson, God has done it again for us. These women has kept a nice house."

They began to look for the bed rooms and found two nice bedrooms.

"We can all get to bed and get some rest. Tomorrow is another day."

Suddenly, a car pulled up pull right into the yard. Someone knocked at the door.

"Why are you people here? This house is for another person. They are moving in tomorrow. They took the mark, and the president promised them this house. Have you all taken the mark?" he said with a smile.

"No," said Paul. "We will not take the mark. We love our Lord."

"Okay, you guys put these so-called Christians in the van."

"Oh no, Dad. Where are they taking us?"

"I do not know, Terry."

They began to push them, hit them, until they got them to the van.

"If you do not take the mark, you will suffer. We have a place for you all in jail. We lock up people that do not take the mark."

"I told you I will not take it. We do not care what you all do. Our Lord will help us. Jesus is coming back. He will take us home."

When they got to the jailhouse, the man said, "We are going to keep you all locked up. That will give you time to think. Look, I took it, and it does not hurt."

"Mister, it will not bother you now. But when you feel the flames of hell, you will get your pain."

"What are you talking about? You shut your mouth." He hit David in his head.

"You will see, God will watch over us."

"But your time is waiting to begin. Okay, little girl, what about you?"

"Like my dad said, I will not take your devil's mark."

"That is okay." He pushed Terry and her dad into the cell, and then he continued talking to the rest of the crew.

Everyone said, "No we will not take the mark. ""Oh, you silly people. You will die soon."

Terry heard the conversation and a tear fell from her eyes.

"We will pray to our Lord. He is here. He said he would never leave us or forsake us. So, Terry, do not worry. God would not want us to. Remember, he won't put more on us than we can deal with.

That night the Christians slept on the jailhouse's hard bed until the next morning.

It is breakfast time and the jailer said "I have two trays, one has bread and you all water the other has eggs, bacon, toast, and coffee. Which one do you all want?"

David said, "It is a trick. We are not going to take the mark."

"Okay, you crazy people. Here is your food: bread and water." He went to the other cell.

"We feel the same," said Paul. "We are not going to deny our Lord. You might as well stop. We are not going to change our minds. Our God will help us."

"Well, that may be right. But you are with us now. We will not give you food the rest of the day."

After the jailer left, the people began to pray. "Dear Lord, help your people. We are crying out to you. Sweet Jesus, we love you."

The next day, in came a man with a knife in his hand.

"Okay, mister. We have given you time to make up your mind. Hold your hand out. You will take the mark or we will take a finger."

"No, Dad."

"It will be okay. Terry, God is with us. Remember the Bible where there were many things happening? Where some people would not deny God and they were put in jail and some were killed? Those people would not give up. So let it be. I will not take the mark."

"Okay then, show me your hand."

So her dad's finger was cut off. The blood was all over David. Terry began to cry.

"Dad, I am so sorry."

"Honey, it did not hurt." But Terry saw tears in her dad's eyes. She put her arms around her dad.

"Okay," said the man. "I will be back tomorrow. No food today, only water. We do not want you to die. You must suffer."

"Dad, it is so bad."

"Yes, dear. Terry, we can make it for Jesus. He died for us so we could go to heaven."

"Dad, they are at the other cell. They are cutting off Paul's finger." Terry and David could hear them crying. "Dad, will it get worse?"

"I am sure it will. But we have God. He is here."

"Dad, if we had been saved, then we would have gone in the rapture. Dad, it says in God's word there will be 144,000 that will come out of the great Judgment. We will have company. Some of them people in Georgia will be with us."

"Terry, tomorrow is your birthday. You will be eleven years old. Yes, look where you will be spending it at. It will not be long. Jesus will come. It will be all over for us. But the ones that take the mark, Lord, what will they do?"

"Dad, let's think of something nice when you were with Mom, before you left."

"Okay, Terry. One day, your mom and I went on vacation. It was a stormy night like it was when you were born. It came up all at once, your mom got soaked and she had to change clothes from her shoes to everything she had on. She was so upset. This happened before you were born. Your mother was so pretty."

"I can't wait till I see her again, Dad."

"Me too, honey. We will all be brothers and sisters."

"You will not be my dad?"

"No, honey, not in heaven. It will be different than on earth."

"Dad, I am going to lie down now. Dad, how is your hand?"

"It hurts a little."

The next morning, the jailer arrived. "Here is your breakfast: bread and water." So the man gives Terry and David their water and bread. The water was hot.

"Tom, I am going to see if we can find any more of them Christians. Will you be okay here with them?"

"Sure, Bill. I will be fine."

There was a window over the room where Terry and her dad stayed.

"Hey, you guys. Look up here."

"What is it, Dad?"

"Someone is outside."

Before they had a chance to turn around, the men were inside. They knocked out the jailer, and unlocked the door for Terry and her dad.

"All of you come and go with us. We have a car outside."

So Terry and the others went with the two men.

"My name is Jim, and this is Sam. We are at a safe place. I see you all have been through so much."

"Yes," said Terry, "My dad lost a finger. He would not take the mark."

"I know already, Terry. God came to me in a vision and told me where you all were. I know your name is Terry, your dad is David, and in the back of the car are the Jacksons and the Owens. I know you have not eaten. So here is some food."

Jim brought them some food—bread, meat, and canned goods. There were other families with them.

"We are all Christians, and God has led us here. This is a safe place."

"Yes," said Sam.

"We have water as much as you need, and we have nice clean beds to lie on.

"Thank you, Lord," said Terry, "for the place and food in the jai l we only had water and bread."

"We have been here for a while."

"We knew there were more of us. God let us know."

"Everyone we need to pray that is the only way we will make it. I did not know it would be this bad. After the rapture, I know Mom told me what would happen because all the love is gone. Only God's people feel love. It is worse now than it was before. It says in the good book it would be that way. My mom took us to church every Sunday and Wednesday night in prayer meetings unless we were real bad sick. My morn loved the Lord."

"My dad did too. My dad passed away when I was little. Mom had to do the best she could. The Stones were known to be in church when the doors open. Now Mom is gone to heaven. She went in the rapture with all the rest. My daughter Terry look in her morn's bed she was gone."

"Paul, will you lead us in a word of prayer?"

"Yes, I will. Dear Lord, we are here together waiting for your return. We will never give into the devil. Nothing they will do will change our minds. Help us, Lord, to do what you want us to do give us what we need to keep us working for you. We are all weak but you are strong. You give us power to move mountains. We all have faith. We thank you for the blood you shed for us all when it comes time for us to go. Help us to put faith in You. We all love You. Amen."

"Now I will read the Bible," said Jim. "God so loved the world He gave His only son that who so ever believe in him shall not parish but have everlasting life. I have a few Bibles for the ones who wants one."

"Thank you," said Becky. "I will read it if I may."

"Sure, you can you can have it if you want it."

"Yes, I would."

"You are smart to read. So how old are you?"

"I am eleven. My Grandmother carried me to church while she was here."

"Yes, she is right," said Becky's mom.

"We were so foolish not to realize what was happening in our family. We should have be better parents to Becky. Then we would have been going to church."

"Mom, don't beat yourself and Dad down. You and Dad got saved and we are together. Now we will make it. God will help us. He is all we have except our Christian friends. We all can pray for one another."

"Yes," said Becky's dad. "We will all stick together. We will have to be wise though."

"You people are living for God and He will keep you safe. Now everyone, let's read our Bibles. If you will go to your Bible and turn to Thessalonians 2, Chapter 3: 'Let no man deceive you by any means for that day shall not come except there come a falling away. First and that man of sin be revealed the son of perdition.' Thessalonians Chapter 5: 'But of the times and the season, brethren ye have no need. That I write unto you for yourselves know perfectly that the day of the Lord so cometh as a thief in the night. For when they shall say peace and safety then sudden destruction. Cometh upon them as travail upon a woman with child. And they shall not escape but ye brethren are not in darkness that day shall overtake you as a thief.'"

"Therefore, let us not sleep as do others, but let us watch and be sober. For God has not appointed us to wrath but to obtain salvation by our Lord Jesus Christ. Wherefore comfort your selves together and edify one another even as also. Ye do and be at peace.

.among yourselves that is so good David God has let us know how easy it would.

Have been.

If we had serve him we all could be in heaven, if we had read our Bibles. Yes Dad. If I had left everything along and listen to Mary,

She was so sad when I never gave her a yes. Answer honey do not worry now.

We will do what God wants us to do yes Dad I want to make God proud of me. so when we.

Get home he will say you have done what I wanted.

Dad you think Mary will know me? Yes sure she will it says in the Bible we will know each.

Other.

Will we all need to rest, Dad goodnight see you in the morning ok dear. Goodnight the next day the paper lay on the ground.

Paul pick it up. Look what is on the front.

What I will read it. To all you so call Christians we are going to find you.

We will look.

At all the houses we know you are hid all at once up pull a car.

Run Terry Dad I am behind you. But a man got them.

Before they got out of the yard, dear lord help us please, we need you.

They put all the ones there in the van. We have a place.

For you all now comes the hard part. For you if you do not take the mark

We will punish you bad.

And you well not escape.

I know what you think. It will not happen. See if your God can get you out of this mess

Terry could hear so much crying going on Dad this is so sad.

Look Dad they are lining them up to shoot them,

I see a pot of hot oil in goes a man. Dad what will we do.

They are trying to make them take the mark, they do not want to.

So much screaming from the people look dad they is the beast.

That they want them to bow down to him.

I will not said Terry I love Jesus too much, he is all I live for,

Ok Mr. we will make you take the mark give me your daughter.

No you will not take my daughter,

It is ok Dad,

I will be ok they cannot make me take the mark. Her Dad keep holding on.

To his daughter.

Let go Dad I will pray to God,

He will help me make it through. By that time you can say good bye to your daughter.

She will do what we asked.

Terry could hear so much crying going on Dad this is so sad. Look Dad they are lining them up to shoot them,

I see a pot of hot oil in goes a man. Dad what will we do. They are trying to make them take the mark, they do not want to.

So much screaming from the people look dad they is the beast. That they want them to bow down to him.

I will not said Terry I love Jesus too much, he is all I live for,

Ok Mr. we will make you take the mark give me your daughter. No you will not take my daughter, it is ok Dad.

I will be ok they cannot make me take the mark. Her Dad keep holding on.

To his daughter.

Let go Dad I will pray to God,

He will help me make it through. By that time you can say good bye to your daughter.

She will do what we asked.

Please bring my daughter back Terry was crying Dad I will pray for you.

My daughter.

Dad I love you love you to my dearest daughter don't worry we will meet.

Again.

And Terry was gone her Dad was crying please God do not let anything. Happen to my child,

The lord spoke to his son. My son Terry will be ok she is a brave girl. My son it will not be long now.

I will come and get these that love me that will give the lives for me.

My son you will give your life for me as Terry will also give her life.

It is getting so close I will not let the devil bother you Are Terry you both are mine.

Forever.

In walks Paul what happen David? They come and got my child. And they.

Will come to get the rest.

Everyone it is time to meet the ant. Christ. He is waiting.

You all will meet the beast,

So that is what they did, David saw Terry with chain on her arms and legs.

He call out to her.

She could not hear him, they had her eyes cover up so she could not see.

But they let her Dad see her how they

Push her to the place where they would take her life

Then they took off her blind foul and brought her dad to where.

She was waiting. Ok you both will die if you do not take the mark.

You can say bye to her Dad I love you we will meet again on the other side I am doing this for Jesus, they had David to tell her bye Terry you are a brave daughter goodbye Dad see you in heaven goodbye my daughter love you.

They shot them both dead. This is the end of my story. "I hope this is not the end for some of you all."

"I hope you are like my Mary and go in the rapture like Mary and her family and friends did."

"I have my home in heaven my name is in the book of life Where is yours at."

—Jeanie Breedwell Dobbs

BOOK 3

To my mother, Georgia Johnson, your memories will always live in the very core of my heart.

Mom, this is your little girl you pray for night and day, The memories come to me as the years slowly pass away. Sometimes the tears fall from my eyes when I start to pray, But, Mom, I am not that little girl; God changed me and took all the burdens away.

No, I am not that little girl, I am not the same anymore. Since Jesus came into my life, I have joy, joy, joy

There is peace in my heart—it is there to stay.

Thank you, Mom, for your prayers;

It turned my life another way.

This story started in a little town outside Chicago where there lived a family of four—Elizabeth; John, her husband; and their two children, Sarah and John Jr. The mother was brought up in a Holy Ghost— filled home. She went to church with the rest of the family. She had two sisters, Glory and Rose. She was named after her aunt Rose because she carried a rose to church.

To the pastor of the church, in memory of his late wife—she loved roses. She had passed away, leaving her husband and two children. They were a young couple. She was loved by many.

Elizabeth read the Bible. She told anyone that would listen Jesus was coming. She and her husband talk of it often. Elizabeth and her family were ready to go.

The Bible is coming true every day. Elizabeth read hers and listened to the news about the government and how things were taking place in Israel. She was on her computer and saw the little children with their heads cut off.

This put tears in her eyes. Dear Lord, please help Israel. Put your angels there for them and other people. Why are they so mean to your people, dear Lord?

Elizabeth talked to her husband. "John, I know Jesus is coming.

"Yes, dear, you are right. Where I work, a co-worker has family in Israel and no one can reach them. It is where so many people are killed. He does not know if they are alive are not."

"John, that is so bad."

"Yes, Elizabeth."

"Why do the people like to follow the devil?"

"I do not know," said John.

"Them people do not like God."

"Yes," said John. "They think they are right."

"They are wrong. They have a big surprise coming to them on Judgment Day."

"Yes, you are right, Elizabeth."

"John, here is what it says in Matthew 24:3-8. These people are talking to Jesus. They said, 'Tell us when shall these things be? And what shall be the sign of thy coming, and of the end of the world? Jesus answer and said unto them, take heed that no man deceive you. For many shall come in my name, saying, I am Christ; and shall deceive many.'"

"And ye shall hear of wars and rumours of wars: see that you be not trouble: for all these things must come to pass, but the end is not yet. For nation shall rise against nation, and kingdom against kingdom: and there shall be famines, and pestilences, and earthquakes, in diverse places. All these are the beginning of sorrows.'

"John, then they will kill you. The Christians will be hated of all nations, and this is because we loved the Lord and we want to follow him. Then because of iniquity, the love of many will wax cold, but the ones that keep God's commandment will be saved. The gospel will be preached all over the world for a witness to all nations after the rapture. Then the great tribulation such as was not since the beginning of the world."

"Immediately after the tribulation, John, this is what is going to take place. The sun will be darkened, the moon shall not give her light, the stars will fall from heaven, the powers of heaven shall be shaken as it was in the days of Noah so shall the coming of the son of man. They were eating, drinking, and merrymaking and giving in marriage until the day Noah went into the ark. Watch. You do not know when the Lord will come.

"John, I have got to make supper. The children will be in soon."
"Elizabeth, do I have to pick them up?"
"They will ride the bus, John."
"Then if you do not need me, I will clean the yard."
"Okay, dear, I do not need you. John, we will have supper at six p.m."
"It is three p.m. I see the kids getting off the bus."
The children made their way to the house. "Hi, Dad."
"Hi, son, how was your day at school?"
"Dad, it was okay."
"We will get off early tomorrow," said Sarah. "Mom, did you wash today?"
"No, why?"
"Because I need my pants. We are going on a field trip next week. That will be on Wednesday. Can you and Dad pick me up?"
"I will, dear. Your dad has got to work."
"Okay, Mom."
"I will be a little late unless things change, and I can let you know. I can wash on Monday. That will be a good day for me."
"Mom, what is Dad doing?"
"He is cleaning the yard for the weekend. Your nana may come over next week. You know how she is about things that are not clean, most especially the yard. Mom is one cleaning person. Your dad does not want to hear her mouth."
"Mom, don't you think it is the wrong time for Nana to come? I thought she would want to come at Christmastime. She never comes in July."
"Well, dear, maybe she is lonesome."
"Yes, Mom, she may be. I do miss Nana. We all used to live close to each other, but when Grandpa passed, Nana moved somewhere else. Why doesn't Nana move in with us? We could take care of her. I was looking at her in church. She did not look too good."
"She is okay, dear."
"Mom, what are we having for supper?"
"Sarah, I made a pot roast with potatoes and some greens I picked up early this week. And some pie."

"That will be good."

"Yes, dear."

"What kind of pie?"

"Apple."

"I like that," said Sarah.

"So does your brother, John Jr. Sarah, your birthday is in December. You were a Christmas baby, almost. Then you will be thirteen. You will be a teenager on the ninth. What did you do at school today, dear?" asked her mom.

"We had spelling to do. The teacher talked about drugs. She was down on drugs. She cannot stand them. It took most of the day. She had people to say what they wanted to say about drugs. I just sat there and listened. I know God does not want people to use drugs, so I did not care to listen."

"But, dear, you need to listen."

"I know."

"I was thinking about the rapture. It is going to happen soon."

"People better get ready, Mom."

"Yes, dear, I agree."

"She did not have time to give us any homework, Mom. Mrs. Green is her name. Do you know her, Mom?"

"Yes, dear. When I went one day, she was there. We talked about you and your studies. She likes you. She said you were a good student."

"That is good, Mom."

"Yes, dear, to have your teacher to like you is very good. Tell your brother and dad it is time to eat."

"Dad and John Jr., Mom said supper is ready."

As Sarah's dad entered the kitchen, he said, "Something smells good."

"Elizabeth."

"Yes? I cooked pot roast."

"Good. I like that."

"I know you do," said Sarah.

"Wash your hands, John Jr."

"Okay, Mom, I will. It will take me a while."

"I know you were playing with them frogs."

"Not this time, Mom."

"After we eat, I need everyone to come to the living room. I have something I need to talk to you about."

"What, Mom?" said Sarah.

"I want to talk about Jesus coming. It is soon. We need to be ready. We need to tell people about his soon return.

"Sarah, do you still talk to Ruth, your friend that goes to school with you? Do you know if she is saved?"

"Mom, she does not talk to me too much. She knows I am a Christian. And she does not want to change her life, Mom. She is fourteen and has got a boyfriend."

"I think that is too young."

"Don't you, Mom?"

"Yes, dear, I was almost eighteen when I met your dad. Mom would not let me date till I was seventeen."

"Wow, Mom."

"She kept a lead on me, she and Dad. We lived in the county, and that was good for them. I had to go to the city to find your dad. Back to Ruth. You need to ask her to go to church with you."

"Mom, we have Wednesday-night service tomorrow night."

"If she wants to go, I will pick her up," said her mom.

"I can ask her at school tomorrow, if she will talk to me."

"It might be too soon."

"If it is, maybe she can go with us on Sunday," said Sarah.

"You can still tell her we have Wednesday-night service."

"Okay, Mom, I will."

"I would hate to know we made her miss the rapture when we could tell her how much God loves her and how bad it will be on earth after the rapture."

"Mom, she does not have a dad. He left her and her mom many years ago."

"That is so sad."

"Yes, Mom, it is. I do not know how I could live without you and Dad.

She and her mom live alone."

"I need to ask my family something."

"What, dear?" said her husband.

"We know Jesus is coming back real soon. I need to know if my family would be ready. So do I have to pray that you all get ready?"

"No, dear, we are all ready." said her husband.

"Mom, I went to stay with Nana, and she read me the sinner prayer. She told me how bad it would be."

"Me too, Mom," said John Jr. "How we do not want to miss the rapture."

"Nana really laid it out for me." she said. "If you take the mark, you will go to hell. So everyone is ready, Mom. Nana carried me to church."

"Now, Mom, are you ready?"

"Yes, children, I am ready. Well, since we all are ready, it is time to go to bed. You all know tomorrow is a school day, and Dad has got to go to work."

"I am going over to North to see your aunt Rose and Tammy, my little niece. Your aunt Rose wants me to take her shopping."

"Mom, are you shopping?"

"I do not know, Sarah. Why, do you need something?"

"No, Mom, I just thought you were going to the dollar store."

"Honey, I do not know where I will be going, but if I do, what do you need?"

"Mom, I need some paper."

"I will pick it up for you and also get John Jr. some candy."

"Yes, Mom. Thanks."

"Sarah, do not forget to talk to your friend."

"Okay, Mom, I won't. Pray for me."

"I will, dear. God can turn this thing around, I am sure."

"Mom, do not forget my candy," said John Jr.

"Wow, look at the time. It is time to go to bed."

"Yes, it is. Good night, Mom and Dad."

"Good night, kids. See you all tomorrow," said Mrs. Moore. "I need to clean the table, then I will go to bed."

The next morning was Wednesday.

"You all get up and get ready for school."

"I am up. Mom."

"Me too."

"Okay, I will have you breakfast soon. John, do you want to eat?"

"No, I am okay. I have got to go. I am running late."

"Okay, dear. Have a good day."

"You too." He kissed her on the cheek before he left. "Everyone, have a God-blessed day."

"You too, Dad," said John Jr. as he entered the kitchen.

"Where is your sister? I thought she was up too."

"She is. Mom."

"Okay, dear, here is your breakfast."

"Mom, I just want a glass of milk."

"You okay, dear?"

"Yes, Mom. I was up most of the night. I was thinking how I was going to ask Ruth to church."

"I see. The only way is just say it. Let her answer."

"She may not say anything, Mom. She does not want to go."

"How do you know that?"

"Mom, I know her. She does not want to give up her boyfriend and whatever she is doing."

"You can take that to the bank."

"Come on, John Jr. Let's not be late. I need to talk to Ruth. Are you ready?"

"I am coming. Oh, I am ready."

"Bye, Mom."

"Bye, kids."

When Sarah got to the school, she saw her friend Ruth. "I need to talk to you."

"About what."

"I know you are older than me, so I know you can make up your own mind. I want to know, do you want to go to church with my family and me? Mom wanted me to ask you. I need to know, do you go to church anywhere?"

Ruth laughed. "What do you mean me go to church? Not me. Anyway, Mom does not go, and I do not go."

"You know, Jesus is coming soon."

"What of it?"

"Ruth. you do not want to be left behind."

"I will be okay."

"You think that, but when it happens—"

"Nothing will bother me."

"Ruth, you are only fourteen years old. You have not lived long enough to make the right choice."

"What do you know about it? You are younger than me."

"You do not have to be old to read your Bible."

"And it is true. I do not want to go to your church. I feel so alone. I have no one. My dad left me when I was a baby."

"What about your grandma?"

"You mean Nana?"

"Yes, that is. My dad, mom, and I do not see her too much."

"Mom will not take me. I know your nana goes. Besides, I have a date Wednesday night. You thank your mom, but it is no deal. I do not think he will want to go. Well, I didn't ask."

"Ruth, it is time to go in my room. We will talk later."

After Sarah got out of school, she went to get her brother. It was an early day. As she entered her house, she called out to her mom. "Mom."

"Yes. Sarah?"

"I did talk to Ruth. She does not want to go."

"I am sorry, honey. Did she say why?"

"She has a date, mom."

"She is fourteen years old."

"Her mom does not care who she goes with."

"That is bad."

"Mom, she did tell me her dad left her mom for another woman."
"That is even worse."
"Mom, it hurt her so bad."
"I am so sorry again, Sarah."
"Mom, why do men want to leave their home?"
"Do not know. Sarah, you have a lot to learn. You have two parents when she only has one."
"There is so much she goes through the kids at school make fun of. And she thinks it is her, the reason they are not living together. She blames herself."
"All kids do. Maybe next week I can go see her mom. I will try."
"That would he good," said Sarah. "Ruth's mom might like that."
"When you go to school, tell Ruth to ask her mom if she would like to go for lunch."
"Okay. I can do that. Mom."
"I do not know Ruth's mom."
"I am sure she could use a friend."
"Yes, Sarah, everyone could use a friend."
"Mom, I am going to clean my room. I have a few things I need to do, put some clothes away and my shoes in the closet."
"Okay, dear. I have got to make supper."
"Mom, could you make us a cake?"
"Yes. I have got some cake mix. I picked it up when I went shopping with your aunt Rose. Yes, I did get your paper and John Jr.'s candy. I put it on my dresser."
"Okay, Mom. Thanks.
"You are welcome. Your dad will be here soon."
"Mom, are we going to church tonight?"
"Yes, we are. Sarah, if your dad gets home. I wish you could have talk Ruth into going."
"Me too. Mom.'"
"She is set in her ways, maybe, like her dad."
"Mom, you did not know them?"
"No, Sarah, I did not."

"I guess I will look in the fridge, see what we have. I need to find something for supper. I was just thinking. Sarah, could you come to the kitchen?"

"Yes, Mom, I am coming. What do you want, Mom?"

"I thought I would call your friend Ruth's mom. Do you know their last name?"

"Hall, Mom. Her name is Judy."

"I will look it up in the phone book. I want to call her. If her daughter is anything like you said she is, she will forget to ask her mom anything. I want to set something for tomorrow at lunch, not wait on her daughter. We may never get to have lunch with her mom."

"Mom, that sounds good. Go on and call Ruth's mom."

"Honey, go on back to cleaning your room."

"Is that all?"

"Yes, dear. Can you tell me where John Jr. is?"

"Mom, I see him outside, playing. Do you want him to come into the house?"

"No, do not bother him until your dad comes home."

"Mom, I am about finished with my room."

"Okay, dear. I will see if I can find my phone book. Here it is. Now her last name is Hall. I will go to the h's. See, her name is Judy. Here it is. I will dial the number."

"Hello, is this Mrs. Hall?"

"Yes?"

"Judy Hall?"

"Yes, how can I help you?"

"My daughter, Sarah, is friend to your daughter, Ruth. They go to the same school. I was talking to my daughter about having lunch with you, and I will be free tomorrow. Would that be good for you?"

"You have something on me?"

"Your daughter has been to my house, but I have never met you."

"Yes, it would be nice to meet my daughter's friend's mom. I like to go eat at the Steak 'n Shake."

"Yes, that would be nice. My daughter said you and your daughter live close to the school."

"Yes, we live on Bay Street, the same side of the school."

"How are you and your daughter doing? I was thinking, Sarah said your husband left."

"Yes, he left us when Ruth was a baby. She only knows he is her dad. He used to come to see her—until he moved. We do not know where. He just one day left, did not say anything."

"He left you for another woman."

"Yes, he did."

"We will talk tomorrow. Have a good night."

"Thank you, Mrs. Moore."

"Bye."

I will pick her up around twelve. That stuck in Elizabeth's mind. I have got to call her back. "Hello, I am sorry, but I forgot to get your address."

"Yes, I thought you would call me back."

"I wanted to tell you I will pick you up around twelve. Your name is Judy?"

"Yes."

"My name is Elizabeth Moore. My name is in the Bible."

"Yes, it is, so is my Ruth's name. You can call me Judy. My address is 408 Bay Street. You cannot miss our home. It is two houses from the school. Blue and white, with a fence so I can keep my dogs inside. Do not worry, they are little babies. They will not bother you. With us living alone, my little Ruth and I feel like if I put the sign up, no one will bother us."

"You are right, Judy. I have got to hung up now. Glad to meet you. See you tomorrow, Judy. I drive a tan car. Can't miss it. My name is on the tag."

"Okay, Elizabeth, see you then."

"Bye now. Let me get busy. I need to get supper done. My husband will be in soon."

She put her food on for cooking. "I need to check on Sarah. She has been in her room for a while."

Sarah had fallen asleep. "Sarah, are you asleep?"

She opened her eyes. "I guess I feel sleepy."

"Yes, I guess you did. I called your friend. We have a lunch date tomorrow at Steak 'n Shake."

"Good, Mom."

"I think that is your dad. I have got to finish supper." As her husband entered the kitchen, she said, "Dear, call your son. He is outside, playing somewhere. He has been there for a while."

"I see him. John Jr., come here."

"I am coming, Dad."

"Look at you. You get to that bathroom, clean yourself up. What have you been doing to get so dirty?"

"Dear, how was your day?"

"Okay, dear John, I have a lunch date tomorrow with Sarah's friend's mom. I called her and asked her to go for lunch at the Steak 'n Shake. I am going to her house. I hope they'd go to church with us this Sunday."

"We have got to hurry. Wednesday-night service. We are going, right?"

"Yes, we are. Okay, I will put the food on the table."

"Then I need to get John Jr. in the bathtub."

"Sarah, you come on. Get ready to eat. We are going to church tonight."

"I will be there in a little."

"Okay, dear."

"Mom, I am clean," said John Jr.

"You get to that table and eat. Sarah, let's get to the dining table."

"Mom, I am here."

"John, will you say the blessing?"

"Sure, dear."

"Father God, first, I want to thank you for dying for us, all the blood you shed for the world. For my job, my family. Lord, there is so much I need to thank you for. Be with my wife when she goes to lunch with my daughter's friend's mom. If she is not saved, save her. Let this day be for my family and for you, dear Lord. Also, be with my children at school tomorrow and be with us at church. Send down that good old

Holy Ghost feeling. Do not let anyone walk out without you as the Lord and Savior. We give you all the love. Bless this food. Amen."

"We have one hour to get ready. I will clean the table." It took Elizabeth ten minutes to clean the table.

"Dear, I am going to gas up. I do not want to run out between here and the church or on my way to work."

"Yes, dear, I would not want you to. Sarah, I hope I can talk Ruth's mom into going to church next Sunday."

"Mom, I wish you could also."

"I hope your dad gets here real soon. I do not want to be late for church."

"Here he comes, Mom."

"Yes, dear, I see him. I have got to see if John Jr. is ready. Come here. Let me check you, see if you are ready for church. You go in that bathroom, clean your ears."

"Okay, Mom."

"I am ready, Dad," said Sarah.

"What about your brother and mom?"

"Mom, are you ready?"

"Yes, dear. Sarah, get my Bible from the bed."

"Here it is, Mom."

"Let's go to the church."

"Hello, Pastor. How are you?"

"I am okay, Mrs. Moore. How are you and your family?"

"Hello, Mrs. Moore."

"Hello, Nancy, how are you doing?"

"We are all okay. It sure has been a pretty weather."

"Yes, Mrs. Moore, it has. I have been real busy. Had to wash some clothes for my family."

"School is going to be out soon. I think this is the last week."

"Yes, Mrs. Moore, it is. My kids will go to stay with my mom."

"Really?"

"Yes, she wants them to."

"Well, everyone, welcome to God's house. Jesus is coming soon. We want to welcome everyone. If you are here the first time, please come back again. We have some cards we need you to fill out. If you came to get fed, put your feet under the master's table. You will leave here happy. For all that need prayer, could you raise your hands?

"Okay, yes, Sister Owens."

"My sister is real sick."

"Okay, we remember these sisters."

"Pastor, her name is Nancy. We wonder if she may go to the hospital."

"Let's remember Nancy. Yes, Sister Williams."

"My lost loved ones."

"Let's remember Sister Williams's lost loved ones."

"Anyone else? Yes, Joe."

"Pastor, my wife is sick."

"Let's remember Brother Joe's wife."

"I see that hand. Yes, Paul."

"My dad. The doctor said he had cancer."

"Well, let's all go to God in prayer. Dear Lord, we come to you with these requests. First of all, we want to thank you for all you have done for each and every one of us. We bring Sister Owens's sister to you, praying you will heal her. And Sister Williams's lost loved ones, Lord. Speak to their hearts and save them. And Brother Joe's wife, heal her from her head to her toes. And, Lord, we know that there is no sickness that you cannot heal. Brother Paul's dad is in the hospital with cancer. We call that by name and tell it to go, in the sweet name of Jesus. Amen.

"Now we will do our singing."

Meanwhile at Ruth's house . . .

"Mom, my friend Sarah asked me to go to church."

"What did you tell her?"

"Mom, I did not want to go to church. Anyway, I have a date tonight. He would not want to go to church."

Ha, I wonder if that is what her mom wants.

"She called me for lunch at Steak 'n Shake. She wants to come and pick me up tomorrow."

"Might be, Mom. Mom, have you ever gone to church? You may have gone when you were a child."

"Yes, I did. Your nana and grandfather made sure we kids went."

"Why don't you want to go now?"

"I do not know."

Back at the church . . .

"We all know Jesus is coming soon. The things that are taking place. You cannot watch TV anymore without someone getting killed. Is the government going crazy? The USA is lost without God."

"Do we have anything coming up for the month of July?"

"We need the ladies to meet in the church next Wednesday."

"Get with Mrs. Williams. She will explain what you need to do."

"Pastor, I need to meet with all the brothers about a fishing trip. It will be in September, but we have got to plan for it."

"You guys see Brother Joe Miller about this. I am sure it will be a nice trip."

"I think he wants to check out Georgia for the fishing trip for all that wants to go."

"I would like that," said the pastor.

"Before we close, I feel like someone needs to make Christ their savior. For all that needs something from, God could you put up your hands? I want to pray for you. I see them hands. Dear Lord, I know you see our brothers' and sisters' hands. I pray for them you will meet the need of your people, in the name of Jesus.

"Now, everyone, come back Sunday morning. Brother Joe, could you say a word in closing?"

"Dear Lord, we want to thank you for this service and for the cross. Keep us safe going home. We give you the glory, and all God's people, say amen."

"Amen."

"Hold on, John," said his wife. "Hi, Sister Williams. How are you?"

"Okay. How are you, Sister Moore?"

"We are all fine."

"I will see you Wednesday night."

"Oh, that is nothing. I just want to get things for a yard sale. We have some time now."

After the Moores got home . . .

"I want to be ready for my guest tomorrow," said Mrs. Moore. "I will study my Bible, some of Revelation and Matthew. It will give me something on the coming of the Lord so I can tell Judy where to read it. I have got that lunch date with Judy Hall tomorrow. She does not talk to her daughter about Jesus. I will pray before I have that lunch. I will let her be the one to talk, ask questions, and I will be ready for her."

"Mom, I am going to bed. See you and Dad in the morning."

"Okay, dear."

"Love you both."

"We love you too, dear," said her mom. "Honey, you have got some pretty hair, so blond."

"Thanks, Mom."

She called out to her husband, "I am going to finish reading my Bible, dear."

"I want to read God's Word. It will make me feel better after the things that went on at work. I hope to rest while I sleep."

While Mrs. Moore was reading her Bible, she heard something in the bathroom. She put her Bible down and went to knock on the bathroom door. "John Jr., is that you?" She knew Sarah was in her room; it had to be her son.

"It's me, Mom."

"What is the matter, son?"

"Mom, I am sick to my stomach."

"Honey, where do you hurt?"

"It does not hurt, Mom."

"Let me pray for you. You do believe Jesus can heal you?"

"Yes, Mom, I do."

"Hold on, let me get the rest of the family."

"I will sit down, Mom."

"John and Sarah?"

"Yes, dear," said her husband. "What is wrong?"

"What is wrong?" said Sarah.

"John Jr. is sick. Let's all pray for him."

"Okay, dear," said her husband. "Let's hold hands around him."

"Dear Lord, I want to thank you for all you have done for my family. Lord, please heal my son John Jr. from his head to his toes. Satan, we come against what you have put on our son. In the sweet name of Jesus, we leave him in your nail-scarred hands."

"Mom, I feel like John Jr. is okay."

"Me too," said her husband.

"I feel like God heard our prayers," said the mother. "John Jr., go to bed. I know you will feel better by morning."

"Yes, Mom, I do believe in Jesus."

"Me too, son," said his mom.

"Good night, Mom and Dad," said Sarah.

"Good night, dear. John, your daughter said 'good night.'"

"Have a good night, dear."

"You too, Dad."

"I am going back to my Bible," said his wife.

"Yes, and I am going back to bed," said her husband.

"It is getting late, so I will read what I can and ask God to help me tomorrow. I am sure God will open my mouth and put words to help Judy understand the Bible."

Mrs. Moore read a few chapters in her Bible and went to bed. While Mrs. Moore was trying to sleep, her husband kept moving around, keeping her from sleeping.

"What is wrong, dear?" He kept on sleeping.

What is wrong with him? Must be having a bad dream.

She had her mind on Judy. She knew that Judy did not go to church. Her daughter, Sarah, told things that she knew Ruth told her. Now Mrs. Moore wanted to change Judy's mind and talk to her about getting saved. She knew all she had to do is plant the seeds and God would water them so they would grow.

The next morning, Mrs. Moore got up. "Dear, are you okay? You had a bad night?"

"Yes, dear. I want to tell you about my dream."

"What dream, dear?"

"When I went to sleep last night, I had a dream about the rapture."

"What did you dream about?" said Elizabeth.

"I heard the trumpet sound. I saw angels. I was leaving my bed, and I saw Jesus—not his face. I was so happy, then I opened my eyes."

"I do not know what that means."

"Elizabeth, he is letting us know the Rapture is very soon. It says in his Word we will know that it is close with dreams and visions."

"You just had a dream. It is going to happen. This world we are living in is so upside down. We are all going though things that God can only make right."

"You are right, dear," said her husband. "I got a call yesterday from my sister Rose. She said there was one of her best friend's son that got killed when a car passed by their house. He was only twelve years old. The person that shot him missed his baby sister lying in her crib. The mother was out other mind. Her son was a good boy, said the newsman."

"John, I have got to get the kids up for school."

Sarah heard her mom. "I am up, Mom."

"Me too," said John Jr.

"Okay, breakfast is ready."

"Bye, dear," said her husband.

"Bye. John, have a good day."

"Bye, kids."

"Bye, Dad."

"How do you feel, John Jr.?"

"Good, Morn. Mom, what is Dad doing in the yard?"

"I do not know. Well, he is coming in. What is wrong, dear? Do you want to eat with the kids?"

"No, dear, I just forgot something. I will see you all this afternoon. Hope you have a good day with Sarah's friend's mom."

"Yes, dear, I will try."

"Well, I better get to work." He left.

"Okay, kids, let's eat."

"Mom, I just want toast and milk." said Sarah.

"Me too," said John Jr.

"Sarah, I will wash after my dinner date."

"Mom, do not forget my pants for the field trip."

"Okay, dear. Put it where I can find them."

"I will, Mom. We are going to school now. I want to get their early. I want to talk to Ruth."

"You all be safe and have a good day."

"Thanks, Mom. Come on, John Jr."

"I am right behind you."

When Sarah got to school, she saw Ruth. "What are you doing, Ruth?" "Nothing at all. Why?"

"I just thought we could talk."

"Does it have anything to do with your mom wanting, to have lunch today with my mom?"

"You do not like that, do you, Ruth?"

"Not really, but my mom has a mind of her own. I cannot change that."

"She does not know my mom."

"True. It is time to go in. I have been waiting for the bell to ring so I call go to my class."

It was lunchtime at school. Sarah got with her friend Ruth. "You know, Ruth, your mom. I am sure, could use a friend. That is why my mom called her."

You are right. She could use a friend. She does not have too many. The ones I know, they drink, smoke, do their thing. My mom does not need that kind of friend. All they want is for themselves. None of them want to help Mom. She has got to work to make ends meet and take care of me. My aunt Brenda, Mom's sister, she comes over now and then. Mom goes shopping with her."

Back at Sarah's home, Elizabeth was washing clothes. She found Sarah's pants and washed them. She looked at the clock; it was time to go. I have got to stop for gas.

When she got to Mrs. Hall's, she knocked on the door. "Hello."

"I see you made it."

In front of her stood a very pretty lady, around forty to forty-five. Her hair was pretty and blond. She was dressed in a blue top that really made the blue of her eyes stand out. The pants she was wearing were black and made her look really small. Her daughter looked like her, except Ruth's hair was black—maybe like her dad's.

Her mom did have a little brown in the front of her hair.

"Come on in. You are Mrs. Moore?"

"Yes, that is right. You can call me Elizabeth."

"My name is Judy. Glad to know you."

"Are you ready, Judy?"

"I need to put my dogs in the house before we go."

"I will wait for you in the car."

"Okay, it will only take me a minute. I will try to rush it. Here I am," said Judy.

"Come on in. It is a little dirty. I will clean it later. Where is Steak 'n Shake at?"

"The road we are on. Go left on Main Street. Go to miles to the red light on the corner of Main and First street. We are on our way."

"What is going on? Lots of cars here."

"Yes, it is."

"We are at Steak 'n Shake, aren't we?"

"Judy, are you ready to order? It is on me."

"I will have a steak burger and large fries."

"Make that two, lady. Judy, you can get our drinks if you want to. I will take a Coke."

"Me too," said Judy.

"We need some napkins too, Judy."

"We can sit here at this table."

"These burgers are really big."

"Yes, Elizabeth, they are."

"Please, could we say the blessing over our food?"

"What?" replied Judy.

"I need to pray. I do not care if we are at home or are in Steak 'n Shake. Does not bother me. I want to thank God. Don't you ever thank God for your food, Judy? Go ahead and thank him."

"What did you want to talk about'?"

"I wanted to know if we could pick you up for church Wednesday night."

"Know what? You hear me, I do not go to church."

"Why'?" Their voices got loud, bothering the ones in the seat next to them.

"Why are you so loud, ladies?" said a girl named Ann.

"We are talking about the coming of the Lord. And he is coming soon," said Elizabeth.

"How do you know that?" replied Judy.

"I read my Bible," said Elizabeth. "I know his Word is true."

The others that were eating went over to get into the conversation. "We are all together. My name is Paul. This is Billy on my right, one of my friends. This is my friend Tommy on the left. We are all in the ball game from Tennessee. We would like to sit in with your all."

"My name is Elizabeth. This is Judy. Her daughter and mine are friends. They go to the same school. We are having lunch. I just met her, called her on the phone. I was talking to her about going to church."

"Lady, why should she go to your church? Could you tell us how you know Jesus is coming?"

"Look at your TV. It is all coming true in the Bible."

"Can you prove he is coming back soon?" said Ann.

"All of you who want to know about Jesus, gather around," said Elizabeth.

"When Jesus was crucified, it was because he loved us and he wanted us to be free from sin. He arose again on the third day. All we have got to do is ask Him to forgive us. John 3:16 says God loved the world so much He gave His only son, that who shall believe in Him shall have everlasting life. Jesus said all who have sinned come short of the glory of God. That is why we have got to confess our sins."

"We understand that," said Judy, "but we are talking about his return."

"Okay, Judy, here it goes. After Jesus's death, he said, when he went away, he would come again to take us home. The ones that put our trust in him live our lives for him. We would go to heaven when the rapture would happen, but if we feel like we do not need to confess, we will not make it in the rapture. If we cannot stand what is going on now, how will we live after the rapture? Do you all not know how bad it will be here on this earth? Jesus says it will be worse than it has ever been. That is why I am ready to go home. So is my family. I want to talk to as many as I can, get them saved."

"Yes, you are right," said David. "Now we need some answer."

"Mrs. Moore?"

"Yes, Tina? It has been a while since Mom told me Jesus is coming. I sit here listening to you and it sounds like you have the answer. What makes you different than my mom? She does not understand why he has not come. You tell us he is coming."

"It says in the Bible it would be like it was in Noah's days. Do any of you young people look at the news?"

"Yes, I do," said Paul.

"I think we all do," said Sue. "Why did you ask?"

"Because it is in the Bible. Everything you see is coming true. Do any of you read the Bible?"

"I used to when I was a child," said Tina. "We were made to go when the church doors were open—Mom, Dad, my sisters and brothers. I told Mom I would never go to church again because we were made to go Sunday morning and evening and Wednesday-night services."

"What about the rest of you? Maybe at one time in your life you read the Bible. God's holy Word."

"That does not tell us anything," said Jerry. Some of the others joined the conversation.

"Has any of you all been saved?"

"What is that?" said one of the guys in the group.

"That is where you ask God to forgive you of your sins."

"Then what?" said Jerry.

"Jesus will forgive you of your sins, and he will take you to heaven."

"How can he be God and Jesus?" said Tony.

"Because he has that right. When he died, that made him God because he came from God. You see one, you see the other one."

"Oh," said Ron, "that makes it sound okay."

"Does any one of you want to give your heart to God? It will only take a few minutes. God loves you all so much."

"How do we confess, Mrs. Moore?"

"For all that wants to confess, repeat after me."

"I am in," said Tina.

"What about the others? You will never be the same. You will be so happy living for Jesus.

"Do not hold back. He wants you to open your door so he can come in. He will take you places you've never been. We are living in the last days. This could be your last time to come to the Lord. He will help you like he did before he went to the cross. He was there for others, healing them, feeding them. All you have got to do is pray, believe in him. Let's say the sinner's prayer.

"Jesus, forgive me of my sins. I believe you died and went to the cross. You shed your blood for me. One day you will come back again. I know that I will be ready to go home. Now, Lord, I do not know these young boys and girls, but you do keep them safe as they go home. Show them that gave their hearts to you a church, and put their names down in the Lamb's book of life. I give them to you. As they did come to me for answers, you told me what to say. In Jesus's name. Amen.

"All that asked God to come into your heart, you need to tell someone. That is what God would want you to do. That you will let people know you are not ashamed of your Lord to confess you are a Christian."

Elizabeth could see tears in some of their eyes. This made her know they had given their hearts to God. "For all that confessed, I want you to have my number. If you need a Bible, I will buy you one. Just let me know. Tina, here is my number. Call me if you need to. Sue, you have tears in your eyes, so here is my number. You can also call me."

"Thank you, Mrs. Moore."

"You are welcome. Before we leave, I want to say a word of prayer. Please, for anyone that did not say the sinner's prayer, do so. Jesus is coming. This could be your last time. You never know God has your number. Get ready. Make it right with your Maker. And you all need to find a church somewhere. Get with God's people. Jesus will help you. Now let me pray for everyone.

"Dear Jesus, thank you for the ones that gave their hearts to you and the ones that did not speak to their hearts. Lord, help them to make the right choice in life, what you want them to do. Let them know you are the only way. Everyone say amen.

"It has been nice to know all of you. Hope we meet again in heaven someday. For the ones that need anything, call me. I will help you and I will pray with you. I love you all. It has been good for me as well. I have got to leave."

"Are you ready, Judy?"

"Yes, I'm going to get home. It has been nice for me too," said Judy.

"Hope to see you all again. I will pray for you all. I have a notebook in my pocket. Put your names and numbers in it. I will have my church to pray for you too. Judy, I will take you home then. I have got to go home. Judy, did you say the sinner's prayer?"

"No. Why?"

"I was praying."

"You did? I do not know what you are talking about."

"If you listen, I will tell you. That is okay, Judy. You need to think about Jesus coming."

"Ever since you have been with me today, you have tried to push your church on me. Now I do not want to hurt you, but stop. I went with you for lunch not to be preached to."

"Okay, Judy, I did what God wanted me to do."

"I am out of here. It has been a nice day. At least some got saved. It was not a lost day. Thank you for the lunch."

"God, he sometimes gives us time to come to him. You remember it could be your last time, Judy."

"Hogwash. I will be okay."

"You have a good week, if you can."

"Thanks. I will try. Got to go. See you."

On the way home, Elizabeth was sad. When she got home, she was happy. God took control. Please help them to live for you. I am glad I gave them my number.

Elizabeth was walking to the house when the phone rang. "Hello?"

"Mrs. Moore?"

"Yes, it is me. Can I help you? Who do I have the pleasure speaking to?"

"Mrs. Moore, my name is Tina."

"Hi, Tina, can I help you?"

"Yes, you can."

"Okay, I am here. Tina, what do you need?"

"When someone talks bad to you, what can you do? I do not have a Bible."

"Tina, I will get you a Bible when I go shopping."

"Thank you, Mrs. Moore."

"You are welcome, Tina. Where do you live?"

"You know where the Burger King is in Highway 401?"

"Yes, I do."

"I live in the blue house behind the burger king. The address is 316 Maple Street."

"Tina, honey, I will bring you a Bible."

"I live with my mom and dad."

I will bring it this weekend it' I can, okay?"

"Mrs. Moore, thank you."

"Tina. keep your mind on the Lord. Do not listen to what they say. You are a very pretty; girl. Those people are trying to find someone to talk about. Pray to God. He will help you. Tina, we could pick you up for church it' you want us to."

"That is okay. Mrs. Moore. My parents go to church. I will go with them now."

"That is good."

"I know they have been praying for me and my brother Tony. My mom and dad always went to church as they grew up. My nana, she carried me to her church. I like it. I seat with the preacher's wife. I visit my nana after Grandpa passed. He went to church with Nana, I remember. I miss them so much. She is gone now. I know one day I will see them again.

"I am glad you called me. You can call me anytime."

"Mrs. Moore?"

"Yes. Tina?"

"How do I pray?"

"Honey, in God's Word. You repeat after me.

"Our Father, who art in heaven, hallowed be thy name, thy kingdom come, thy will be done, on earth as it is in heaven. Give us this day our daily bread and forgive us our debts as we forgive our debtors, and lead us not into temptation, but deliver us from evil for thy is the kingdom and the power and the glory forever. Amen."

"Is that it, Mrs. Moore?"

"Yes. Tina. God does the rest."

"That is easy."

"Tina, don't your mom and dad have a Bible?"

"Yes, they do, but I want one to call my own."

"I see."

"Nana gave me one, but I lost it. We moved a lot, and I cannot find it. Mrs. Moore, do you think Jesus is coming soon?"

"Yes, I do, Tina. So much has happened, and it is all in the Bible."

"Mrs. Moore, after the rapture, what will happen?"

"It is going to be real bad, Tina. No one will be able to live on this earth. Tina, do you have time?"

"Yes, Mrs. Moore. I want to understand so I can tell people, my family, that aren't saved so they won't be left behind. My brother Tony, he is living like the devil sometimes. His wife, Peggy, does not see him for days. When he does come home, he looks like he has not slept in days. Peggy thinks he is on some kind of drugs."

"I need to talk to him. Tina, tell him about the mark of the beast."

"He does not talk to my mom and dad. We have talked, but that was before I got saved."

"Tell him if he does take the mark, he will go to hell. He cannot change what he does."

"I am so glad I said the sinner's prayer."

"Me too, dear. You take care and call me when you need to."

"Bye, Mrs. Moore."

"Bye, Tina."

For the ones that read this book, please read the first and second book God gave me the words to write. I pray before I write. This could be true. I am not saying it is, but I feel like God gave it to me anyway.

Are you homeward bound? Jesus is coming. About the rapture, the second is after the rapture, the third after that.

Now it is time for Elizabeth's kids. They are coming home from school. After Elizabeth got in, she heard Sarah's voice. "Mom, are you home?"

"Sarah, she is here. She drove her car in the back," replied John Jr.

"Okay. Mom, we are home."

"Yes, dear, I will be there in a little." "Okay."

"Where is your brother?"

"He is behind me."

"Here I am, Mom. I was in the kitchen."

"Change your clothes, John Jr. You can wear them tomorrow."

"Mom, the weekend is here," said Sarah. "How was your lunch with Ruth's mom?"

"Honey, you are not going to believe this. Let's wait until your father gets in, then I can tell it only once."

"Okay, Mom. He will be here soon."

"Mom, Dad is home."

"He must have gotten off early."

"Mom, he is coming in."

"Give him time, kids. Give him time to catch his breath, Sarah."

"I will, Mom."

"What is going on around here?" said Mr. Moore.

"Dad, Mom had lunch with my friend's mom, and something happened. She wants us to hear it at the same time."

"I need to wash my hands first. Have some oil on them."

"I bet you are tired, Dad," said Sarah.

"Not too tired. I want your mom. If she has time, I am ready to listen to what happened today."

"John, I will be there in one minute. I need to start supper first. John Jr., I told you to change your clothes."

"I will, Mom. Wait on me. I will change real fast."

"All right, let's all gather in the living room. It will be a while for me to tell you what went on at Steak 'n Shake. You all know I had lunch with a lady named Judy, who is Sarah's friend's mom. I called her yesterday. This was before we went to church. I was motivated when the night came about. I had read my Bible, and I was ready for Judy. God helped me to read and understand his Word, so I knew how to handle what she said. I picked her up around lunchtime. When we got to Steak 'n Shake, there were lots of cars in the parking lot. The reason was lots of kids in the ball game were having lunch with cheerleaders. Also, John, do you know where Steak 'n Shake is at in town?"

"Yes, I do."

"That is where we were at. I got to talking to Judy. She got really loud. It brought all them kids to where we sat. They all started asking questions, and I told them about Jesus's coming. They wanted to know more, so I told them what God gave to me. To make the story short, some of them got saved. John, Judy lives next to the school.

"Going back, the lunch was on me. Judy got our drinks and napkins. A girl named Ann was sitting in front of us. That was what started it all. I felt like a preacher, listening to what their minds were on. It sounded like an open book. I was so glad to help them. I did not know they were so interested in the Bible. To me, they wanted to know about the Bible, and I was the one to answer all of them. It was one after another.

Wanted me to help them. I do not understand why no one helped them in their young lifetime.

"John, these kids were really young. Made me think of our own kids. And if the Lord does not come for a while, where would they be? It is something to think about."

"You are right, dear. We are up in age. Our children could be left alone after we go."

"What would happen to them? With no one to help them, they may marry some bad person that could lead them on the wrong road. The kids, I told them all I could about the Bible."

"Yes, Mom. Then what happened?"

"I told them it says in the Bible it would be like it was in Noah's days when Jesus comes back. Some of them got touched, like Sue, Tina, Ron, Tommy, and a few others."

"Then what happened?" said her husband.

"I asked them if they wanted to say the sinner's prayer. Tina, a little girl, she was really small. You could see the tears falling from her eyes. She wanted to know the Lord. Some of the others were crying also. You could tell no one had talked to them. I felt sorry for them.

"Tina is seventeen. She did not look it. Very pretty girl, long brown hair, it covered her face a little. That was the way she wore it around her pretty face. The rest were not to worry like Tina. She touched my heart. Tammy was really tall, with long blond hair really big blue eyes. She did not talk to me. I did give them all my phone number. I asked them, what if they were left behind? I saw their faces. They were scared.

"After we got Through, I said a prayer for them. They all bowed their heads. I drove Judy home. She still does not want to change her life. I dropped her off, and I came home. I got a call from Tina just as I came into the door. She was so upset. The kids were mean to her. I think they found out she got saved, and they did not like it. I told her they just wanted to pick on someone and they found her. I told her to pray about it. She asked me how I lead her in the Lord's Prayer. She said it sounded easy to her. I told her I would go shopping and buy her a Bible. She liked that. I asked her to go to church on Sunday. She told me she would go with her parents. They both go to church. I said that it's good. She was happy to go with them."

It was time for bed.

"The phone is ringing, Sarah. Will you get that?"

"Yes, Mom."

"Hello?"

"It is Ruth, Mom."

"I wonder what would make her call us so late at night. What happened?"

"I am sorry to call, but I had no other one get to me."

"What are you saying? Mom, she is crying."

"Give me the phone. What is the matter?"

"I found your number. That is why I called you."

"What is wrong, dear?"

"Could you take me to the hospital? My mom ran into another car. Mrs. Moore, could you take me to see my mom?"

"Yes, dear, I will be there in a little while."

"John, I need to take Ruth to the hospital. Her mom had a bad accident. The police called her after it happened."

"How is her mom?" said Sarah.

"I do not know. She does not know."

"I will go with you, Elizabeth. I do not want you to go by yourself. The kids will be okay while we are gone. I am ready if you are. Sarah, we will lock the door when we leave."

"How is her mom?"

"She does not know, John. Look for her house. It is close to the school."

"There it is, Elizabeth. She is standing outside."

"Come on, dear, and get in. Ruth, she will be okay. We will pray for your mom."

"Mrs. Moore, do you think she will make it? The way the police talk, she is really in a bad condition."

"Honey, she is in God's hands. He will have the last words. Maybe she will change her mind about him."

"Mom has been upset this week. I think she has been talking to my dad. I have been worried about her."

"There is the hospital. You can park over there. This is Sarah's dad. John, meet Ruth."

"Glad to meet you. Mr. Moore."

"Sorry about your mom."

"Thank you, sir. We can go in this door. I will find my mom."

A lady saw Ruth. "Can I help you?"

"Yes, please, my mom, Judy Ann Hall."

"Let me check. Okay, honey, you go sit down Arc these people with you?"

"Yes, my friends."

"I need to talk to them. Her mom is really bad. We do not look for her to live.

"John, how do we tell her that?"

"Can we see her?"

"Hold on. I will be right back. Are you their kin?"

"We just want to pray for Ruth's mom."

"Okay, you all go first. I will stay with the daughter," said the nurse. "She is in that room."

"Mrs. Hall, I am Mrs. Moore. We had the lunch, remember? How do you feel? She is not responding, John. Dear Lord, give her one more chance. She needs to give her soul to you. Look, John, she is moving. God answered my prayer. Mrs. Hall, are you okay? She is trying to move her lips. I need for you to repeat after me.

"Dear Lord. I am a sinner. Please forgive me of my sins. I believe in you, and I thank you. Amen.

"John, she will go to heaven."

"Doctor, Mrs. Hall is coming around," said the nurse. "Call her daughter. She wants to see her."

"John, go get Ruth. Her mom is asking for her. Do not tell her she is dying

"Wait. I am going to."

"She is in the waiting room."

As Elizabeth and John were leaving the room, Ruth was on her way in. Elizabeth reached out to her. "Honey, she is awake now. She is asking for you.

Ruth began to cry.

"She is all right with Jesus."

"What are talking about? I thought you all were praying for Mom."

"We did."

"I am sorry, Mrs. Moore. I am worried about my mom."

"Honey, go to her. She needs you. Ruth, she will be different. She said the sinner's prayer. Now when she goes, she will be ready."

"Thank you for that news. Mrs. Moore."

"You are welcome. God did it. Look, John, she is holding her mom."

"I see. Let's go get some coffee. Looks like we will be here for a while."

"Okay, let's see if Ruth needs anything. Ruth, do you want anything?"

"I will be in the waiting room," said John.

"Did you get to talk to your mom?"

"I need to talk to them. Her mom is really bad. We do not look for her to live.

"John, how do we tell her that?"

"Can we see her?"

"Hold on. I will be right back. Are you their kin?"

"We just want to pray for Ruth's mom."

"Okay, you all go first. I will stay with the daughter," said the nurse. "She is in that room."

"Mrs. Hall, I am Mrs. Moore. We had the lunch, remember? How do you feel? She is not responding, John. Dear Lord, give her one more chance. She needs to give her soul to you. Look, John, she is moving. God answered my prayer. Mrs. Hall, are you okay? She is trying to move her lips. I need for you to repeat after me.

"Dear Lord. I am a sinner. Please forgive me of my sins. I believe in you, and I thank you. Amen.

"John, she will go to heaven."

"Doctor, Mrs. Hall is coming around," said the nurse. "Call her daughter. She wants to see her."

"John, go get Ruth. Her mom is asking for her. Do not tell her she is dying."

"Wait. I am going to."

"She is in the waiting room."

As Elizabeth and John were leaving the room, Ruth was on her way in. Elizabeth reached out to her. "Honey, she is awake now. She is asking for you.

Ruth began to cry.

"She is all right with Jesus."

"What are talking about? I thought you all were praying for Mom."

"We did."

"I am sorry, Mrs. Moore. I am worried about my mom."

"Honey, go to her. She needs you. Ruth, she will be different. She said the sinner's prayer. Now when she goes, she will be ready."

"Thank you for that news. Mrs. Moore."

"You are welcome. God did it. Look, John, she is holding her mom."

"I see. Let's go get some coffee. Looks like we will be here for a while."

"Okay, let's see if Ruth needs anything. Ruth, do you want anything?"

"I will be in the waiting room," said John.

"Did you get to talk to your mom?"

"Yes, Mrs. Moore, I did. She is resting now."

"Do you want to go with us?"

"Yes, I will be there one minute."

When Elizabeth entered the waiting room, she said to her husband, "John; she is resting. Ruth is going with us. Here she comes now. She will need someone to lean on. That will be us.

"Come on, Ruth."

"Mrs. Moore, do you think Mom be okay?"

"I do not know. I only let God make that decision. I think she is left in God's hands. I may be wrong. I always let God take care of things that are too big for me. We did pray for your mom. Ruth, what can we get for you?"

"I would like a Coke. I do not like coffee."

John only got two cups of coffee and one Coke. "Do you want something to eat, Ruth?"

"No, I am okay. I am worried about my mom."

"We can go back now. John, lead the way."

They had just gotten in the waiting room when the nurse came out. "Your mom needs you."

In Judy's room. . .

"Mom, I am here."

Her mom looked up at her. She saw the tears in her mom's eyes. She knew it was time for her mom to go. Ruth tried to hold her tears back. She began to shake. Her world was about to end, the memory of her dad leaving and her mom telling her she would take care of her now resurfacing. She was so lonely without him. Now she had to let her mom go. She said to herself, "Please do not take my mom. I will be all alone." She did not know where her dad was.

"What do I do?" The tears fell from her eyes. She could not hold back.

"Yes, Mom."

"Honey, Mom is going home to heaven. You be a good girl."

"No, Mom, don't leave me."

"Honey, God is calling me home. I am sure the Moores will let you stay with them."

"I will go get them. Come with me, Mrs. Moore, and bring your husband."

"What is it, Ruth?"

"My mom is telling me good-bye. She said she is going home to heaven." Elizabeth could see the tears in Ruth's eyes. "Honey, it will be okay. You can stay with us."

The nurse called them back. "Would Judy Hall's daughter and friends come to her room?" Judy rose.

"Elizabeth, please take my daughter. Take care of her. God is calling me home."

"Oh no, Mom, you cannot leave me!" She was getting really loud. "Please, Mom, do not go." Then Ruth looked over her mom's bed and saw an angel look at Mrs. Moore.

"What, honey?"

"I see it." Ruth saw her soul leave her body. "They come to take your mom home."

As the tears fell from Elizabeth's eyes, she hung on to Ruth.

The nurse had to give Ruth a shot. "This should help you. Her mom had gone."

Elizabeth knew if she had not gone to the hospital, Judy would not been saved. She was so happy. "Well, John, another has gone home. We need to get Ruth and go home. Her mom is gone."

"Yes, dear, I will carry her to the car. Here she comes."

"She is okay," said the nurse. "We gave her a shot. It has helped her to settle down. Here is some more. Make sure she gets one when you think she needs one. It has been a while. You can give her one when you get home, but give her something to eat."

"Thank you, nurse."

"I know she can use support from you people. God will bless you for what you have done. I believe you both just came into her life."

"Yes, we did. We will be there to help her has much as we can. Her mom wanted us to help her."

Ruth was still crying. Mrs. Moore put her arms around her. "Let's go home."

"You folks drive safe."

"Thanks. We will. Ruth, we will be home soon. Lie back, we are on our way.

It was around 4:00 a.m. when John, Elizabeth, and Ruth got home. John opened the door. "You have the key?"

"Yes, dear, I do." They knew the two kids were asleep, so they walked slowly through the house.

"Come with me, dear," said Elizabeth. "You can sleep in the guest room. Hold on, I need to give you one of your pills. I will give you a breakfast bar. You are supposed to take it with food. Are you all right? Do you need to talk about anything?"

"No, ma'am, I am okay, just tired. I do miss my mom. She was so good to me since Dad left. She stood in for him too."

"Here is your blanket."

"Thank you."

"Sleep good." said Mrs. Moore. She could hear Ruth crying. She gave her a hug. "Honey, if you need us, we are here for you. Your mom would not want you to cry. She is in God's hands now. We have plenty of room for you. Good night."

After she said "Good night," Elizabeth went to her room. "John, she is crying."

"She will be okay."

"We will pray for her. She will be with Sarah tomorrow."

"You mean today."

"Yes, dear."

Elizabeth had not closed her eyes when she heard her children talking. Elizabeth got up, went to the kitchen, where her kids were.

"Mom, why is Ruth sleeping in the guest room?"

"Honey, she is an orphan."

"What?"

"Yes, her mom passed away. It was after we got to the hospital. She did not live long, but not before she said the sinner's prayer."

"Mom, that is so good."

"Sarah, she is in heaven. Yes, Sarah, but I feel sorry for Ruth. She has been through so much, with her dad moving out. Now she does not know where he is. She will stay with us for a while then. I do not know what she will do. She is a child without God in her life."

"She does need moral support. We will do that for her after school. I will talk to her. She can go to church Sunday. Mom, I know what time you all got here. The car lights woke me up. You need to lie down for a while. I will get John Jr. up for school."

"No, honey, I will be okay. I can sleep after you all leave. Your dad is really tired."

I guess I better call John's office, let them know what happened. I am sure they will understand. "Honey, get your brother up for school."

"Mom, do not make breakfast. I will get John Jr. and me something."

"Okay, dear, I will call your Dad's job." Elizabeth dialed the number.

"Mr. West, this is Mrs. Moore."

"Yes, dear."

"I am John Moore's wife. I have some very sad news."

"Is John okay? What about the kids?"

"We are all okay. John is tired. One of our friends was in a wreck. We were at the hospital all night. She passed away."

"So sorry, Mrs. Moore."

"Anyway, we got home at around four this morning."

"That is okay. Tell John to rest. I will see him tomorrow."

"Okay, Mr. West, he will be there. Have a good day Mr. West."

"You too, ma'am."

Elizabeth hung up the phone.

"Sarah, hurry. You will miss your bus. You tell Ruth's teacher she will be back at school, and tell them her mom passed away. John Jr.?"

"Yes, Mom."

"Hurry."

"I will be finished in a little."

"Okay, dear. I will see you both after school."

Sarah kissed her mom. "Okay."

They left. "Bye, Mom."

"Bye, kids. I will read my Bible now."

Jesus is coming soon. It says so here in God's holy Word. All the things it says, it has happened.

She fell asleep. Her husband woke her up. "Are you okay, dear?" said John.

"I am okay. I was reading my Bible, fell asleep. I know we all were tired, but we feel better than our little guest. She feels so alone without her dad and mom."

"Have the children left?"

"Yes, dear, they have."

"I need to call my work."

"Too late. I did it for you. Mr. West said for you to rest."

"Thank you, dear, that was nice of you."

"John, I am going to check on Ruth. She was asleep a minute ago. She may be up because I heard someone. She may need something. She does not know where things are.

"Ruth, are you up?" said Elizabeth.

Yes, I am. Come on in. It took a while for me to go to sleep thinking about my mom. Mrs. Moore, my mom and I have always been together. It is hard for me to live without her, except staying with my friends. Mrs. Moore, I will need to find out when they will bury my mom. My mom has a sister over in North, Aunt Brenda. She well be the one to take care of the arrangements."

"I will call the funeral home to see if she has gotten in touch with them."

"Mrs. Moore, she does not know about Mom. We are the only ones at the hospital."

"Do you know her number?"

"I do. Mom gave it to me one day. Here it is She is home right now. She is off on Friday."

"I will call her if you want me to," said Elizabeth.

Ruth dialed her aunt's number. Her aunt Brenda answered, "Hello?"

"Aunt Brenda." Ruth was crying.

"Is something wrong, dear?"

"Aunt Brenda, I need for you to come see me.

"Where are you at?"

"I am at my friend Sarah's home."

"Okay, dear, where is your mom? I have not heard from her so long. I pray for you both. Is your mom with you?"

"Aunt Brenda, here is my friend's mom. She can tell you the address and how to get here."

"Hello, my name is Elizabeth Moore. We live on 401 Highway. We live in Tennessee. Call us when you get close. I will meet you."

"Okay, good, I am on my way."

"Ruth, she is on her way. She will call when she gets on 401 Highway. She said to tell you she loves you."

The phone rang about one hour later. "We are on our way."

"Ruth, your aunt is waiting at the station."

"I did not want to tell her about Mom on the phone."

"She and my mom were real close at one time, but when Aunt Brenda changed, I did not know at that time. Now I do. Aunt Brenda must have given her heart to God because she said she has been praying, for Mom and me. She must have told Mom. They did stop talking."

They were waiting on Highway 401 for her aunt when someone drove up beside them. "That is my aunt."

"We will wait till we get to the house. She is behind us."

"Get out, Aunt Brenda. This is Elizabeth, my friend Sarah's mom."

"Glad to meet you."

"Aunt Brenda, Mom is gone. She had a wreck, hit another car."

"I am sorry, dear."

"But she was ready. Mrs. Moore led her in a sinner's prayer."

"I have prayed for that to happen."

"I will go with you, Aunt Brenda."

"Can I get you anything to drink?"

"No, that is okay."

"Your sister went happy. She wanted Ruth to stay with us. While you were on your way, Ruth was getting ready to have her things so she could go with you. She wants to be with family. She said she would have you to take her to her nana. She thinks her nana may know where he is. I told her if she ever needs anything, call us. I told her Sarah will be looking for her. She said she would come to see us when she buried her mom. While we were on the road, I offered her a Coke. She did not want one. She saw you coming. So I am sorry about your sister. She died in the hospital. We were there, my husband and I."

"Did my sister say anything?"

"Not much. She was hurt too bad. As I told you before, I led your sister in a sinner's prayer."

"Mrs. Moore."

"Yes."

"I do not know what my niece told you, but my sister, we had not talked in a while. She found out through me I gave my soul to God. She did not like it. I knew I had to keep her and Ruth in my prayers. She changed when James left her, was going out drinking, and living it up with her so-called friends. James's mom took Ruth for a while because she stayed away a lot. I know Ruth does not like for anyone to talk about her mom. I was saying to her she may be taken and not have a chance to get saved. She did not want me to say that. Mrs. Moore, I have been serving my Lord for a while. I have prayed for my sister many times.

"I do want you to stay with me, Ruth. I will take care of everything. Your mom gave me the insurance policy so when she went, I could take care of everything. I want the best for your mom."

"Mrs. Moore, you and your family are welcome to the funeral. I will let you know when Aunt Brenda and I want to go see Nana."

"We can go there now. It is on our way to the house."

"Do they still live at 427 Highway?"

"Yes, Aunt Brenda. They have not moved yet."

"Mrs. Moore, it is so nice to meet you. Thanks for all you have done for my family."

Elizabeth hugged Ruth. "You take care and come back to see us. I will tell Sarah what you said. I know she will want to see you when she comes home. You all have a safe trip."

"Bye, bye, Mrs. Moore." They left. "Aunt Brenda, I miss Mom."

"Come close to Aunt Brenda. Honey, if you get right with the Lord, you will see her again."

"Aunt Brenda, it has been a while since I saw my dad. I think Nana will know where he is. This is the road, Aunt Brenda."

"I know, honey, we are close to the house."

"Aunt Brenda, do you have a Bible?"

"I do, but I want to buy you one."

"Thank you, Aunt Brenda."

"Here we are, Aunt Brenda. There is a car I have never seen before. I see Nana." Her heart started beating fast. It had been so long since she had been there. She was glad to see her nana. When she got to her, the tears began to fall.

"Child, what is wrong?"

"Nana, Mom is gone."

"She left you alone?"

"No, Nana."

"What do you mean?"

"She had a car wreck. Nana, she died at the hospital last night."

Her nana hugged her. "I am so sorry, honey. Do you want to stay with Nana?"

"Nana, have you seen Dad?"

"Yes, he is in his old room. I will get him."

"Dad."

"Ruth, what are you doing here?" He hugged her. "I have missed you so much. Where is your mom?"

"Dad, I have been trying to tell you, Mom is gone."

"What are you saying?"

"She hit a car and she passed away."

"Come on in, Brenda. Sorry about your sister."

"Yes, I miss her so much. It had been a while since I had seen her and this. . ." She had tears in her eyes. "If it is okay with you, Ruth is going to move in with me. I will take care of her. You can come to the funeral if you want to."

"Sure I do."

"I will do everything, Mom. It is close now."

"Are you living with Nana, Dad?"

"Yes, I got a job. It is close to your Nana's. I do not want her to live alone."

"I miss you, Dad. Maybe I can come see you more now. I will have Aunt Brenda to bring me. I will have to change schools."

"You will be okay, dear. I will go with you to school, get you signed in so you can start right away."

"The house will have to be sold."

"I know, dear. I have the deed on your mom's house. She only trusted me to take care of it, and it is safe where I can get it."

"You can visit your dad anytime and your nana on the weekends. She will like that. And your dad can come see you if he wants to."

"I will like that, to stay with Nana. We do lots of things together. I missed that."

"I have lots of things your mom wanted me to take care of. My name is on the bank account too. She did put her faith in me to take care of everything."

"Aunt Brenda, I do have a boyfriend."

"Honey, you have plenty of time to have a boyfriend. You do not need one now."

"Aunt Brenda, I do need to call him and tell him bye."

"Here is my phone. You can call him."

"We do not have any man coming to our house—nothing serious, Aunt Brenda, just a friend. Mom knew about him."

"Give me the phone. You can call when we get home."

"Dad, we have got to go. I will see you real soon." Her dad was holding on to her. "Love you, Dad."

"Love you, Ruth."

"Bye, Nana."

"You take care."

"I will, Nana. Got to go stay with Aunt Brenda now."

"You be good to your aunt. Come back to see us. Here is my cell number.

Call me."

Back at John and Elizabeth's. it was time for the kids to come home from school.

"Mom, we are home." said Sarah.

"I am in the bedroom. I will be out in a little."

"Mom, where is our houseguest, Ruth?"

"Honey, she called her aunt, and she came and picked her up. Her aunt Brenda is from Nod."

"Mom, I thought she was going to stay with us."

"She was. She wanted to see her family, live with them."

"I know, Mom, but I was hoping she would be here."

"Honey, she is going through so much, with her mom gone. Her dad left first, now she lost her mom. They were really close. I think that is why she did not mind her having a boyfriend."

"Yes, Mom, I guess you are right. She is holding lots inside."

"She was supposed to go to her nana to see if she knew where her dad is."

"I am sure she does."

"He may be there staying with her. If so, she may have a new light on life.

"Mom, I do not know what I would do if it were you."

"Mom, where is Dad?"

"He went to the store. He will be back in a little. Honey, why don't you call Ruth? She will be at her aunt's house. What about the boyfriend?"

"I think they were just friends, Morn. She is moving in with her aunt. She won't see him anymore."

"Her aunt Brenda loves the Lord. She has a different life than Ruth's mom."

"Wow, is that true?"

"Yes, Sarah, it is. That is what she told me. She was glad her sister was saved. She said she had been praying for her. She was glad she was in heaven."

"That is so good, Mom. Mom, I see Dad. He is home."

"Okay, dear. I have got to make supper."

"Mom, do you need help?"

"Honey, I can do it."

In walked her dad.

"Mom said you were at the store."

"Where is John Jr.?"

"He is playing in his room."

"John Jr., come here. I have you something."

"What, Dad?"

"Remember you told me you would like to have a knife? I got you one."

"Thanks, Dad."

"John, are you sure you want him to have that?"

"Elizabeth, I had one when I was a young boy. It will not hurt him. I will talk to him so he will only play with it by himself and watch how he uses it. He is a smart boy."

"John Jr., I would not get you something like that, but I guess it is okay. Your dad trusts you with it. Do not cut your hand."

"I won't, Mom."

"Elizabeth, have you heard from Ruth?"

"No, John, we have not. I told Sarah to call her. So far, I do not believe she has. Ruth's aunt said she would let us know what day the funeral will be. We will wait."

"I know Ruth must be feeling bad."

"Yes, John, I am sure she is. She has got to change school. Sarah will have to see her before she moves so she will know where she will be staying. I guess she and that boyfriend will be over."

"Mom, they were just friends. She told me after her dad left she needed someone to talk to. It stayed with her, him leaving like he did. One day she met this guy."

"Well, family, we need to keep our minds on the coming of the Lord. So much is going on this earth."

"I need for all of you to come and eat. I am going to bed early tonight."

"Mom, you sure need to rest," said Sarah. She was worried about her mom since what happened to Ruth's mom. It was strong on her mind. "Did you ever close your eyes?"

"Just one minute while I was reading my Bible. I will get some sleep tonight. Tomorrow is Saturday. We have lots to do. Your dad has got to work. He will be off at noon. We can all clean the house. No school, so you can help me get our house in order. It is time for bed."

"Mom, supper was good. I like green beans. The beans were good."

"I like canned beans."

"The pot roast was good too, so was the apple pie."

Sarah, you can use the phone to call Ruth. There number is on the phone. Call it."

"Hello, Mrs. Bates."

"Yes?"

"Is Ruth there? I am her friend from school. My name is Sarah. My molt said you came and picked her up. She is staying with you."

"Ruth."

"Yes, Aunt Brenda?"

"Someone is on the phone for you. Here, take it. See who it is."

"Hello?"

"Ruth."

"Yes?"

"It is me. This is Sarah. I am so sorry for your loss."

"Thank you."

"I am sure she will be missed by many."

"Yes, Sarah."

"I know I will miss my mom."

"I wish you had stayed with us."

"I wanted to, but Aunt Brenda wanted me to stay with her. You know family. She carried me to see Nana. And guess what?"

"What?"

"My dad is staying there. I have not seen him and Nana in a while, and it has helped me, with Dad back in my life. Mom would not let me see that side of my family. They were so happy to see me."

"What about your aunt Brenda?"

"She does not mind. She told me I could see Dad whenever I want to and Nana too."

"How is your dad doing?"

"He has a job. That is one reason he is staying with Nana. Sarah, he gave me his cell phone. That way, I can let him know how I Am."

"That is good, Ruth."

"Also, Aunt Brenda will take me to see him whenever I want to go."

"How are you?"

"I will be okay in time, I think. I do miss my mom so much."

"When is the funeral?"

"We will find out Monday when Aunt Brenda calls."

"So you will be selling your home?"

"Yes, I will. That is another thing Aunt Brenda is taking care of."

"I will miss you at school."

"I will miss you too. Aunt Brenda is putting me in a school here in Nod."

"What about Charles, your boyfriend?"

"He was never my boyfriend."

"I bet he will miss you."

"I will call him tonight. He was just a close friend."

"I have got to go. You take care and call me. Let us know when your mom will be put away. Do not take anything that you do not want. Love you, girl.

"Love you too, Sarah. Bye."

"Bye, Ruth."

"Mom, I talked to Ruth."

"How is she doing, Sarah?"

"Mom, she is missing her times with her mom. Mom, she had her aunt Brenda to take her to see her Nana, and guess what?"

"What?"

"Her dad is staying there."

"Did she get to see him?"

"Yes, he was there. He gave Ruth his cell number. She can keep track of her dad."

"That is so good."

"You know, Mom, Ruth missed her dad. Her mom and dad did not get along. Maybe they can get a place together."

"Yes, you are right. Since her mom is gone, they need each other."

"Mom, I am going to bed."

"Me too, dear."

"Your dad and John Jr. have gone to sleep. They have been in bed awhile. See you in the morning, dear. I will pray for Ruth. God can help her if she will put her faith in him. She needs him now more than anyone. Did her aunt say anything?"

"No, Mom. She answered the phone and got Ruth on the line."

"You were talking to Ruth all that time?"

"Yes, Mom. She was talking about James, her used-to-be-nothing. There she told me what I already knew. It was just close friend. One thing more, she needs to go to church."

The next day was Saturday. "Mom, are you up?"

"Yes, dear. Why?"

"Where is Dad?"

"You remember I told you he had to work till noon? He will be in soon."

"Yes, Mom. It skipped my mind."

"Well, dear, we all have things on our mind."

"Mom, did you get any sleep?"

"Yes, dear, I did. I feel better than I did yesterday. God brought me through a lot. I felt like Ruth and her mom were part of our family."

"Mom, I feel the same. I have gotten real close to Ruth since she lost her mom. She needs a lot support."

"We are supposed to do that in Jesus's name. That is why he saved us, so we could carry on his work. And Ruth needs us. We have got to do what God wants us to do."

The phone rang.

"Sarah, answer that."

"Okay, Mom. Hello, Nana?"

"Yes. Sarah, how are you doing?"

"I am okay. Just got up."

"I need to speak to your mom."

"Mom, Nana."

"Hello, Mom."

"Yes, dear. How are you? I called to see if I could come to your house Monday."

"Sure, Mom. You come on. I was waiting on your call."

"Mom, how will you get here? Mom, is Tony bringing you your grandson?"

"Yes, dear. He will be calling me."

"I would like to see my brother Roy and his wife, Linda."

"Tony will bring me after work."

"Okay, Mom. Mom, by the way, can you make that trip next week? We had something happened. One of Sarah's friend's moms died, and we have a funeral we will have next week."

"Yes, dear, I can wait."

"Mom, there will not be anyone to stay with you because we will all be there."

"I understand."

"Mom, I am sorry. I would like for you to come stay with us, and I am sure the rest of the family would too."

"Elizabeth, I can go stay with your brother Roy and Linda. They have been after me so much. To stay with them now would be a good time."

"Are you sure, Mom? I did not think you got along with Roy's wife."

"We do now. She is real sweet to me."

"Okay, Mom. We will talk later, Mom. Love you."

"Love you too, Elizabeth."

Sarah said, "Mom, here comes Dad."

"Mom, I have got to go. John is home from work. Mom, I will call you next week. Bye, Mom."

"Bye, dear."

"John, did you have much to do at work?"

"Not too much. I had a call from your best mother-in-law."

"Yes, the only one."

"She wanted to come for a visit."

"I hope you told her what happened."

"Yes, John. She was okay with it. She will come the second week of July."

"That will be good. Is Tony bringing her?"

"Yes, he is. He is the only way she has to get here other than the bus. You know how Mom hates to ride the bus. Also, my brother Roy got hurt, and Linda does not drive, not too much from the house. Tony takes Mom everywhere she wants to go. He does not mind."

"That is good. I have lots to do. My bedroom needs cleaning."

"Do you need help, John?"

"You work. I was not talking about me. I was thinking about our daughter."

Elizabeth laughed.

"No, I will be okay. I will finish our yard," said her husband.

"Sarah, you have to do some cleaning in your room. It's a mess."

"No, Mom."

"Yes, it is. I was in it while you were at school. I would not want to sleep there. Now you get to work. You have lots to clean. Pick up things."

"I will, Mom,"

"Now, Sarah, not later. John, are you still in the house?"

"Mom, he went outside."

"John, come here."

"Dad, Mom wants you."

"I am coming."

"Come here, John, close the door."

"What is it?"

"I want you to see something. I have Sarah's birth certificate in my hand. I was looking at it. Look, John, should we tell her she has another mother? That we are not her true parents?"

"I do not think she could take it."

"I will put it back up so she can wait a while, not now."

"We love her as much as we do her brother. We could not have a child.

We wanted one so bad. That was all we knew to do."

"I am going to put it in my dresser, under some things, until I can put it away. Here is the Bible I want to give Tina. I have had it for a while. It is new. I'll leave it here where I can find it. Next week I will give it to her. You know, John, tomorrow is Sarah's birthday. That is what her birth certificate says. July the sixth. She will be fourteen years old. That is why she is so smart. Not thirteen like we thought."

"Wow, I did not know. I guess they did not tell us the truth. I have got to tell her, her birthday is not in December. That is the first time I noticed that."

The phone rang.

"Hello. Mrs. Moore?"

"Yes?"

"It is me, Tina. I need to come to your house. I need to talk to you, please."

"Do you have a ride?"

"Yes, a friend will bring me. We are here."

"Is anything wrong?"

"I just have so much on my plate I need to talk about it. Did I call at the wrong time?"

"No, dear. There's so much going on. My daughter's best friend's mom passed away. She has been with us after it happened. Now she is staying with her aunt over in Nod. It hit the daughter real hard."

"Sarah, would you please come here? I have someone I want you to meet. She called me and is on her way here."

"Who, Mom?"

"Remember Thursday I had lunch with Ruth's mom?"

"Yes."

"One of the cheerleaders' names is Tina. She got saved, and she called me the same day we all had lunch. Now she is on her way here."

"Okay, Mom."

"I have something I want to give her. It is on my dresser. Will you go get it, dear?"

"Yes, Mom."

When Sarah pulled out her mom's drawer, she pulled out her birth certificate. "What is this?" She looked. "Wow, it's me. They are not my parents. Why did they lie to me?" She looked at the name Sarah Jean Williams, born July 6. Sarah was so weak. "What is this about?"

With tears in her eyes, she read the certificate. "Linda and Roy Williams are my parents. That is my uncle and aunt. How could this be?" She ran to the front door. No one saw her leave. She went to the library and looked up the date of her birth.

"Wow, tomorrow is my birthday. Not thirteen, I will be fourteen."

She looked for the address of her mom. She had grabbed some money for a cab. She knocked on the door. A blond-haired woman went to the door.

"Can I help you?"

"Yes, I need to speak to Linda Williams."

"It's me."

"How could you do that to your child?"

"What are you talking about?"

"I am your child."

"You better come in. Can I get you anything?"

"No, I need some answers."

"Okay, sit down. I will try to help you. Are you Sarah Jean?"

"Yes, it is me."

Her mom hugged her. "How did you find me?"

"I found my birth certificate by mistake where she left it. I went to the library, looked you up."

"You do not know how many times I have prayed for this to happen."

"Why did you give me away?"

"Honey, I was only fifteen years old when you were born. My mom and dad made me give you up. I am sorry. You do have good parents. They were checked out."

"Why did they not tell me about you?"

"I do not know."

"They had me as a Christmas baby at thirteen years old. I will be fourteen tomorrow."

"Yes, you are right. My aunt and uncle have the same name as yours."

"I thought they were my parents. They did not let me see you after you were born. Does your family know where you are?"

"No, they do not. I left after I found the papers."

"Don't you know—"

"They are out of their minds."

"Let me carry you home. We can still see each other if it is okay with your mom and dad. Maybe later, honey. It is getting late. You do not need to walk. I will be glad to take you home back to Elizabeth and John."

"Where is Sarah?"

"I do not know."

"Let me see. Oh no, she found her birth certificate."

"Let's go look for her."

"I do not think she found Linda?"

"I do not know. I she goes to Linda, I am sure she will bring her home."

"John, we should have told her. She knows everything by now."

Back at Linda's ...

"I cannot believe they did not tell me about my dad."

"Honey, I do not know where he is at. We broke up before you were born. I never saw him again."

"I want to find him."

"Okay, I will look for him. You are a Christian?"

"Yes, I am."

"So am I. We have something to talk about."

"Yes, we do. My parents are Christians also. They take my brother and me to church."

"I heard the reason they have you."

"Why?"

"Because Elizabeth could not have children."

"But what about John Jr.?"

"It happened years later, after they got you, Sarah. I know they love you. They are that kind of people. This is a mess you need to talk to them. You can come see me anytime you want to. Can I take you home? You need to be good to them. They chose you for a daughter. That is better than having you. I wish I could have raised you, but I am glad they did. You were raised in a Christian home. Some kids do not get that. My mom and dad wanted you in a nice home. I think they had them checked out so they knew you would be raised right. They loved you, I am sure."

"You can carry me home if you want to. What do I say?"

"Honey, I am sure they will tell you everything so you will understand. Let's go."

"Do you live alone?"

"Yes, I do."

"Maybe I can come and spend the night."

"I would like that very much, but you will have to make it okay with your parents."

"We are here." Out came Elizabeth and John. "Honey, are you okay?"

"Yes, Mom. Linda told me what happened. I cannot blame you and Dad for wanting a baby. Mom, this is Linda."

"Yes, we meet again."

"She is so pretty. I prayed she would come to me, and she did. I will leave and let you all talk. Sorry, Elizabeth."

"You should know how I feel."

"Yes, I do, Sarah. If you want to see me, if it is all right with your parents, I will come pick you up."

"It is okay," said Elizabeth and John. "Anytime she wants to visit you, she can. We hope she does."

Linda hugged Sarah and left.

"She is nice."

"Yes," said Sarah. "Mom and Dad, I need to talk to both of you."

"Okay, we are ready. Sarah, forgive your dad and me for not telling you about your birth. I was going to tell you, but I was worried that you would not understand. I need to tell you something. They did not tell us the truth about your birth. Today was the first time I saw the papers. So I thought you were born in December, not July. Now we have a birthday tomorrow. Your brother will like that. When I found your birth certificate, I was looking for the Bible. I will tell you the truth. I did not want to tell you about Linda."

"Mom, she is a Christian, and she loves me too. We talked for a while. She said nothing but nice things about Dad and you. She was the one who told me how nice you two were. Mom, she is not what you may think she is. She just wants to know part of my life, and I know you and Dad can share me. There is plenty to go around."

"I know, dear. You can visit whenever you want. Your dad and I have loved you from the first day we brought you home."

"We did not want to share you with anyone. You were our little baby. We did want to keep it a secret."

"That is right."

"Yes, dear," said her dad. "We did not know how much you could love a little baby that you did not give birth to."

"Dad, Mom, yes, I can forgive you. God, forgive me for all my sins. You both wanted me so much. Does my brother know?"

"No, honey, he does not."

"Can we keep it that way?"

"Are you sure that is what you want? He is your brother, just like we are your parents. He may want to know while he is little."

"Mom, Dad, tomorrow we can tell him."

"We are having your party tomorrow. You are growing up."

"Yes, Mom and Dad. I am glad I found out. I do not love you all any less than I did yesterday. You both are great parents, and no one can chime that. It came from your daughter's lips."

"We thank you. You are great too," said her dad. "One thing about it, we know now that you really love us since you already found out about your birth."

"It has not changed anything, Mom and Dad. I thank you both for everything."

"Let's go to bed."

"Good night, Mom and Dad. I mean it, I love you both."

"We love you too, dear."

The next morning was Sunday, a special day for Sarah. She knew who she was, and it was time to start a new life. She had other ones in her future. Something happened to her while she slept. She had a dream about the rapture. She saw Jesus in the dream.

"It is time to go, my daughter. You are a good girl for all you have done. Your mom and dad are Elizabeth and John Moore. Linda is the one that gave birth to you, but she saw lots of angels coming to take her home." Sarah jumped up and ran to her mom.

"What is wrong, dear?"

"I had a dream that Jesus told me Linda gave me birth but you both are my parents. What does that mean, Mom?"

"Honey, I do not know. We will talk about it later."

"Mom, today is my birthday. My real birthday."

"Yes, dear. Your real birthday."

"Sarah, what are you talking about?"

"John Jr., come with me. Mom and Dad, we need to tell him."

"Okay, dear, we will. John Jr.?"

"Yes, Mom?"

"Honey, when your dad and I got married, we wanted a child so bad."

"What are you saying, Mom?"

"Let me finish."

"Okay, Mom."

"Since we could not have a baby, we adopted your sister. The doctor said I could not have one on my own."

"Mom, I thought Sarah was my sister."

"She is, but your dad and I did not have her."

"How did this happen?"

"Honey, it is a long story. We will tell you more later. Maybe you are too young to take this all in."

"I do not care how you got her. She is my sister and will always be."

"We love her has much as we do you. Don't you?"

"Yes, Mom."

"That is how I feel. We got her when she had just been born, so she has been with us since she was a baby."

"John Jr., your sister's birthday is today. She is not thirteen, but fourteen. We had another day, but now we know different. Now you can say 'Happy birthday' to your sister."

"Happy birthday, Sarah," said her brother.

"Thank you, little brother."

"Sarah, we have a surprise for you. Dad got it for you when you went to Linda's house. Close your eyes. Hold out your hands. We know you will be graduating soon. We bought you this dress. Hope you like it."

"Mom, Dad, it is so pretty. Thank you both."

"We have another surprise from your little brother."

"Sis, close your eyes."

"I knew you were getting money. Here is my present, a pocketbook."

"Thank you, little brother."

"We also have party for you. Come on, everyone."

They made their way into the house. Each one of them brought Sarah a present. She got clothes, shoes, many other things.

"Wow, this is so great."

"Hold on. We have one more surprise," said her mom. "Close your eyes." Linda, her real mom, came in with a present—a pretty watch.

"Mom, can I see you?"

"Sure."

"Thanks. I need to ask you something."

"What?"

"Can I call Linda my second mom?"

"If that is what you want."

"Yes, Mom, that is what I want."

"Linda, Sarah wants to call you her second mom."

"That is okay with me."

"Okay, Second Mom thanks for the watch."

Then the party was over.

"Sarah, your dad and I want to talk to you."

"Yes, Mom."

"We love you and want you to know you mean as much to us as your brother, John Jr."

"I know, Mom and Dad."

"There is something else."

"What, Mom?"

"If you want to go to your second mom after school is out, you go with our blessing."

"Thank you, Mom and Dad. I know it took something for you both to give in. That makes me proud to have parents such as you two."

"I know you are."

"Not only thinking of yourself but of others."

"Now we missed church, so what we need to do is gather around the table, and I will read the Bible to my family. We all know Jesus is coming soon. All the signs are in his Word. Be sure when you go take Jesus with you, let your light shine so everyone can see the Lord is the one you live for. Tell someone about Jesus."

"Yes, Mom," said Sarah. "I told Ruth about Jesus. She did not care to hear me.

"Sarah, you need to pray for your friend and at your school."

"Everyone, it is time to eat. We all need to get to bed."

"Mom, did Tina come to the house?"

"No, she never did, but she will call me another time." The phone rang.

"Sarah, would you answer the phone?"

"Yes, Mom. Hello?"

"Is this the Moore residence?"

"Yes, who is speaking?"

"My name is Paul. Can I speak to Mrs. Moore? We met at the Steak 'n Shake. She told us about God."

"Mom, it is Paul. He said he met you at the Steak 'n Shake."

"Okay, dear. I know who he is."

"Mrs. Moore."

"Yes."

"My name is Paul. I had the pleasure of meeting you Wednesday at the Steak 'n Shake."

"Yes, I remember you. Can I help you?"

"The crew all want you to come and speak at one of our churches."

"How is everyone doing?"

"We are all fine."

"Paul, you remember I was with a lady named Judy?"

"Yes, I do."

"Well, she did not get saved the day I talked to everyone. After I left her, she had it had car wreck. Her daughter called me. My husband and I hurried to pick up her daughter. We were there long enough for me to lead her in a sinner's prayer."

"Did she die?"

"Yes, Paul, she did. You never know when God will call you home."

"That is right," said Paul. "We all need to get into God's Word."

"Now, Mrs. Moore, we all vote you as our speaker. We like what you said. There is going to be lots of our friends there. We want them to hear you. They need God in their hearts."

"Where is this place at?"

"We are on Highway 327 off of the lake. The little white church set off the road."

"Yes, I will come. I cannot let you all down. If I was voted in, it must be real important to all of you. What time, Paul?"

"We are going to be there around six p.m. on Wednesday, the ninth."

"Could you be there a little early?"

"Yes, we can."

"I will bring my family."

"That is good. We are looking forward to meeting your family."

"Will the others, your friends, be there?"

"They will."

"I need to call Tina. By the way, have you heard from her?"

"Not since a few days ago."

"Do you need prayer?"

"Yes, Mrs. Moore."

"Dear Father in heaven, we bring Paul and all the others to you, asking you to help them as they do your will. Lead them to the right way. We ask this in the name of Jesus. Amen."

"Paul, you have a good night. We love you all. Keep Jesus first. Good night to you."

"And yours, Mrs. Moore."

"John, that was one of the guys I met at the Steak 'n Shake. He called me to see if I would go to their church Wednesday night to speak about Jesus and the Bible. It is on 427, lake. You remember the little white church set off the road?"

"Yes, I do. What did you tell him, dear?"

'I accepted the offer. He was so happy I said yes. They voted me in, the crew did."

"That is so good, dear."

"I told him about Judy. I know he felt sorry about her being gone. Sarah, I hope you had a good birthday."

"Yes, Mom and Dad. I want to thank you both for making it possible for the children here to celebrate my special day."

"John, we will all go to the church Wednesday night. I need support. I have never done that before. I know God will help me through it all. I have lots of Bible-studying between now and Wednesday night."

The next day was Monday. Sarah got up. Her mom was in the kitchen. "Good morning, dear. Did you sleep okay?"

"Mom, since Sunday, things have changed. I am one year older. Last week, I did not know I would be that old."

"Honey, that is not old."

"Yes, it is, Mom. I went from thirteen to fourteen in one day." Her mom laughed. "And also a different month."

"I get your point, honey, but you are still our little girl. And we love you. That will never change."

"Yes, Mom, I see that. I know Linda now and there is some new people in my life."

"Honey, we know things have changed."

"I know, Mom, and I love you and Dad so much. That will never change. We all can share each other. That is what God would want."

"Sarah, it is time for you and John Jr., your brother, to get ready for school."

"Yes, Mom. Mom, has Dad left already?"

"Yes, he had to be at work early."

"I am ready. Mom, I need to ask you something."

"What, dear?"

"Should I tell Ruth about it?"

"Honey, that is up to you."

"That is my mom."

"Is that what you want?"

"I believe she would understand. I am glad I found out before I got grown."

"Yes, dear. Is John Jr. up?"

"Yes, Mom. Here I am. Ha, old girl."

"You talking to me?"

"Yes, I am. You are old."

"Mom."

"You cut that out, John Jr. Your sister is not old."

"Mom, I was only kidding her. I did not mean anything about what I said. Sarah, I am sorry. I was just picking at my loving sister."

"Okay. It's okay. Let's go, John Jr."

"I am right behind you."

"Bye, Mom."

"Bye, kids."

After the kids left . . .

"I need to study God's Word for Wednesday night. I have never done this before, so I need to pray about it.

"Let God lead me in what to say, dear Jesus. I need your help. I need to lift you up in front of them children and lead them to you. I never have done this before, as you know, so I need everything you have for me to bring them to you. In the name of Jesus. Amen. Thank you, Jesus."

When Elizabeth got up, she felt better. "I believe I can do this with God's help. He is always here when I need him. Now I will read my Bible and pray God will use me for his glory. Wednesday, I will lead the young people to Jesus. That is what Paul said they all need. He is a smart man. Thank God for him."

Elizabeth was thinking about what happened. Now she did not have to tell Sarah about her birth. Maybe God wanted Linda in her daughter's life. She did live for God, and she had prayed he would send Sarah to meet her. Sometimes things work out differently from what we understand. We just have to thank God and go on with our lives. "That is what he would want," said Elizabeth.

The day went by fast. Elizabeth was working on her little crew to come home when she got a call from Ruth.

"Hello, Mrs. Moore."

"Yes, dear. How are you?"

"Fine. Still missing Mom."

"Yes, dear, I am sure you are."

Aunt Brenda wanted me to call you and let you know the funeral will be Thursday. It will be at the Church of God in Nod on 301 highway. We will have the viewing at five p.m. and the funeral Friday at ten a.m. Mom will be buried at the garden. And my dad will be there. I called him, I le said he would be at the church."

"Dear, we will see you there."

"Are you okay? We missed you."

"Ruth, Sarah told your teachers. They were sorry for your loss. They will see you when you come to get your things."

"Thank you, Mrs. Moore. Give your family my love. See you all Thursday."

"Okay, dear. You take care. How is your aunt? I am sure she is missing her sister."

"Yes, I hear her at night, praying for me."

"She loves you, Ruth."

"I know, and I love my aunt too."

"You need to help her as much as you can. Did you call your friend James?"

"Well, his name is Charles James. Some call him James. Me, I call him Charles."

"Bye, Ruth."

In came the children.

"Sarah, that was Ruth. She said to give you her love. She is missing all of us."

"How is she doing, Mom?"

"I guess okay, after what she has been through."

"I know, Mom. I do not know how she has made it."

"Our dear Lord was with her. She told me when her mom would be buried. On Thursday is the viewing. She will be put in her grave on Friday."

"Are we going, Mom?"

"Yes, dear. We have got to support Ruth. She needs us now. She will be at the garden in—"

"Mom, is that where our family is?"

"No, dear, it is a garden. Peace is where our family is buried. She will be in Nod. Our family is not from there."

"Glad you told me."

"Where is your brother at now?"

"Mom, he is in his room. He is playing."

"Mom, Dad is home from work," said Sarah. "That is good, dear."

"How is all my family doing?"

"We are all okay, Dad,"

"That's my girl. Where is my son?"

"In his room, Dad."

"No, I am not, Dad."

"Ha, son. How was school?"

"Okay, Dad."

"I need to talk to my family. Can I get your attention?"

"Yes, dear."

"Okay, kids. Dad has something to ask of us."

"What, Dad?" said Sarah.

"If it isn't a bother to you all, I would like to see my family when I come into the house, unless you have something more important than me. You all know, when I come home, try to meet me at the door. I miss you guys while I am working. I promise not to keep you too long. I just want to see my family for one minute. Okay?"

"That is okay with us all, dear. We will do that."

"Thank you all."

"We are going to the viewing of Ruth's mom on Thursday, and they will bury her Friday. Ruth called me today to let us know."

"Okay, dear."

"Can you get off work on Friday at ten a.m.? They will do the viewing at five p.m. Thursday."

"I will try. I am tired. I want to lie down till supper."

"Too late, John, supper is ready. Let's all eat and go to bed."

Everyone slept real good. It was over, and it was morning.

"Time to get up."

"We are up, Mom. I am dressed for school. Come on, John Jr., we need to hurry to get to school."

The day at school went by fast. They were home again.

"Mom, we are here. I see Dad."

"I have been reading my Bible. I can do a good job for my Lord and Savior. There are going to be lots of people there. I want to give a good speech."

In walked Mr. Moore. "Well, I see my family are waiting on me."

"Yes, dear, we did not forget."

"Good. How is everyone doing?"

"Good, Dad. You okay?"

"Yes."

"That is good," said Sarah.

"Now you all can do what you want to do. Just wanted to see you all when I get home. And you did not let me down."

"We are all going to the church Wednesday night."

"Sarah, they are young, not teenagers."

"That is okay, Mom."

The next day was Wednesday. Mrs. Moore was getting excited. She was going to be the speaker at the church, talk to the young people.

"Sarah, it is time to go to school."

"Short day, Mom."

"Yes. Where is your brother, John Jr.?"

"He will be here in a little."

"Did you both eat?"

"Yes, Mom, we did. I let you sleep in. I thought you may be tired. I am old enough to make breakfast now."

"Thank you, dear. See you both after school."

"Bye, Mom."

"Bye, kids."

Sarah saw Ruth. She came to pick up her things. "Ha, Ruth, how are you doing?"

"I am okay. Aunt Brenda is in the car. She brought me here. She is putting me in school next week. I told everyone 'Bye.' They all did hate to see me go."

"Me too, Ruth. You will be missed."

"But I get to see my nana and dad. Now that helps missing Mom."

"I am sure it does."

Home from school . . .

"Time to go to church. I need to be there early."

"Okay, Mom."

"Do I look okay?"

"Mom, you will make them take notice. It is almost four thirty. Look at your watch."

It took some time to drive. "We have made it. Wow, lots of cars."

"Mom, here come some of the people."

"My name is Paul. Glad to meet you."

"Paul, my name is Sarah."

"Paul, these are my two children, my son, John Jr. You met my daughter. This is my husband, John."

"Glad to meet all of you," said Paul. "You all have a seat. Mrs. Moore, you come with me, You are our guest."

"Where did all these people come from?"

"When you said you would be here, I called lots of my friends.

"Now it is time to begin. My name is Paul. We do have a treat for you all tonight. We have a guest. We know she has her Bible in her brain because this lady got me to take another look at my life. And, others, when I call your name, please stand up. We will do the cheerleaders first. First, Tina, would you please stand up? Stand up, Sue, stand up, Jan, June, Jean, Tammy. These were not saved until this sweet lady followed God's demands and they got saved.

"We love this woman. She has been a blessing to us all. Some of us did not get saved that day, but we are now. Would the boys stand up as I call your name? Tommy, please stand up. Jerry, stand up. David, Lewis, Billy, Ron, Glen, Tommy, and Tony. These are the guys that got saved. This lady is sent by God. I want you all to welcome our guest, Mrs. Moore. Welcome to our church."

"Thank you all so much. You know I felt so special when Paul called me to come to his church. I am so glad to be here. My family are here with me. My loving husband that always shows me support, John. My wonderful daughter, Sarah, also supports me, and last but not the least, John Jr. 11e brings up the crew. I want to thank Paul for wanting me to say a word to all you nice people. God is so good. We all know he is coming back soon. I am here to lift up Jesus to help people get saved.

"I do not know what to say except Jesus loves you all. I am so glad God made a change in your lives, and he wanted me to lead you all to him. I just followed what God wanted me to do. When I met Paul and the others, Tina and some of the young ladies, we all had food at the Steak 'n Shake. I invited one of my daughter's friends' moms for lunch. God had other plans. 1 wanted to tell her about Jesus. Her name was Judy Hall. That was when we all got together. Paul and all his friends joined us to talk about Jesus. There is a sad story to this. I did not know I would see Judy on her deathbed. That same night, her daughter called me. She had a car wreck and passed away.

"She was so bad from the accident we could not talk to her. My husband and I prayed for her. We asked Jesus to give her another chance, and he did. She said the sinner's prayer. God saved her. She went to heaven last Wednesday night, a week ago. You see, people, you do not know when your time comes. God has your number. He had hers. Because Jesus used me, she is dancing with the angels. Her daughter is fourteen years old. She is staying with her aunt here in this town somewhere. She was our guest that night. Brenda, her aunt, carried her home with her. I do not know where you all stand with God. There is a place to make him your Lord and Savior.

"Could we have someone to play one of the songs I really like, 'Jesus will be with you at the cross'? As the song is playing, would you all search your hearts? Give it all to Jesus. He is waiting on you. I have been blessed here tonight. I want to thank you all for inviting me to this church. I must leave. First, let me pray for you all. I want to pray for this church.

"Dear Lord, I want to thank you for all these people that want to follow you, make you their Lord and Savior. Keep them safe on their way home till we meet again in heaven. Amen.

"If the rapture happens, where would you be? God bless you all. Hope you make Jesus your Lord and Savior."

As they were going home . . .

"Mom, I think you did okay. You got the message across."

"I hope I did, dear. We made it home. It is time for bed. John, carry your son in. He is asleep."

"Okay, dear."

"Tomorrow is Judy's viewing."

"What time, dear?"

"Five p.m., dear."

"Okay, I will try to be home early. We need to get some rest."

"John, could you come here?"

"Yes, dear. What do you need?"

"Could you zip me down, dear?"

"This dress is pretty. Is it new?"

"No, dear. I just saved it for times like this."

"Oh, well, you look good up on that stage."

"Thank you, dear. I will try to wear it more often."

"Yes, dear, you do that. We have got to get some sleep. It is late."

The next morning . . .

"I need to put my dress in the washer. You all need to get ready for school."

"Mom, we are ready. See you this afternoon."

Elizabeth read her Bible. She got a call from Ruth. "Mrs. Moore?"

"Yes."

"I need to let you know Mom will not be buried. She is going to be cremated."

"What are you saying?"

"My aunt has business in Chicago. It is something that has got to be done. I will see you all when we get back. I think it has got to do with Mom's things. Love you, Mrs. Moore."

"We love you too, dear."

"Tell Sarah I love her too and I want to see her when we get back."

"Dear, it is time for the kids."

"Mom?"

"Yes, dear?"

"I am home."

"I will be there in one minute. Where is your brother? I hope he is home by the time your dad gets off work. We promised we would be here waiting on him. I got a call from Ruth. They will not bury her mom. They are going to Chicago. They have got to leave right away."

"So they are going to have her cremated? That's bad."

That is what it is. She told me to tell you she loves you and she would see you when gets back. Maybe she will tell you more then."

"Mom, we have one more day till the weekend."

"Yes, dear."

The night went by fast. Sometime that night, the rapture took place. The bridegroom came for his children. The ones that were ready heard the trumpet.

The Rapture of the Church

As it happened, the car that Ruth was riding in went out of control. Her aunt Brenda heard the trumpet call, and Jesus went and got her. Ruth had just woken up. The car had rolled into the ditch.

Ruth looked for her aunt, calling out to her, "Aunt Brenda, where are you?"

Did she fall out? Nothing else came to her mind. What is happening? She saw cars running into each other, planes falling out of the sky, sparks on houses. Then it came to her—the rapture. Her aunt had been ready, but not her. She remembered Sarah talking to her about the Lord coming.

"Why did I not listen?" She began to cry. "What will I do?" They were close to her nana's. She began to push her way through all the things that had happened. She was scared. "Maybe Nana will be home—no." That terrible thing came to her mind.

Nana was ready. People lay all over the highway. Strange. No one was helping them. She kept moving on, crying.

She almost got hit by a pole a car hit. "My, what am I going to do? I wonder if Sarah is home. No, she went in the rapture. I thought I had plenty of time. I have got to find my dad. I wonder if he will be at Nana' s."

When she reached the porch, she saw her dad. "Dad, what has happened?" Her dad had tears in his eyes. "Honey, your nana tried to warn me about this. I did not listen."

"Is Nana gone?"

"She is. I woke up after it happened, looked in her room. All I could see was her Bible, her clothes lying on her bed."

"Dad, it is so bad out there."

"Honey, it will get worse. Mom—your nana—said not to take the mark."

"Dad, my aunt is with her sister now. She has got to be happy. I know I would be to be with Mom."

"Dad, I will not take the mark."

"Honey, we will have to pray for each other."

"Dad, we need to give our hearts to God."

"Dear Jesus, I am a sinner. I am so sorry that I did not serve you. Please forgive me of my sins and welcome me into the kingdom of God. Thank you. In the sweet name of Jesus. Amen."

"Dad, we are saved. We need to get to the others."

"Ruth, you are right."

"Dad, Aunt Brenda and I had started to Chicago. She had things to take care of It could not wait. We were close when the rapture happened. Our car ran off the road. Aunt Brenda was gone."

"I knew it would happen.

"Ruth, your nana carried us to church when we were all little. I knew better than to not get ready."

"Me too, Dad. Many times, people told me the rapture was going to happen. I just did not want to listen. My aunt was getting me a Bible before this happened. Dad, God gives us plenty time to get ready."

"Sorry, dear, you can have your nana's Bible if you want it."

"Dad, let's go in and see what is on TV, see what is happening."

"This is channel 3 out of Chicago. Something really bad has happened. The phones are ringing off the hook. Let me answer this call. Hold on, lady. Do you know what has happened?"

"Man, I cannot find my baby girl. She is gone."

"Lady, stop crying. I am sure there is a reason your child is gone.

"The news is that millions of people are gone. No one heard anything.

Anyone that has an answer to this, please call the number on the screen. We need to know some answers. Cars are all over the highway. No lights, just in some place. Most are in darkness, except some in the county."

"Dad, we have lights, but for how long?"

"I got my TV for fishing and hunting, but we never used it till now. I will try my cell. Hello? My name is James Hall. I can tell you what happened."

"What happened? This is channel 3 News out of Chicago. My name is Paul King. Now, how do you know what happened?"

"I just do. If you had read your Bible, you would too."

"What are you saying?"

"I am telling you the rapture happened. Jesus came to get His bride."

"Who told you this?"

"No one. I believe the Bible."

"You think something happened another way?"

"How do you think we got here? Do you not believe anything about Jesus? Were you never told about Jesus? Did you not go to church? I was dragged to the church. I did not want to go. They made me, mister. I am telling you the truth. Jesus came just like he said he would when he went away."

"Well, if you believe, why are you still here?"

"You know, that is a question I am sorry I can't answer."

"Why not?"

"I do not know. My mom took me to church, but I thought I had plenty of time. I did believe, but I was hoping it would be longer. It was a surprise to me when it happened. My mom is gone. I live with her. We ones that are left behind do not know it, only the ones that are ready.

"Hello? He hung up on me, Ruth. He does not believe me."

"Dad, you will run into people that do not want to face the truth."

"I am going to lie down. It is getting late. We need to rest. You can sleep on your nana's bed."

"Okay, Dad, I will. Say good night."

"Good night, little girl."

The next morning, Ruth heard her dad in the kitchen.

"We need to find some of the others that believe in God because we do not need to be alone, Dad."

"I will see if I can find some things to take with us. Nana has some dresses. She was real small. It may be a little big, but better than nothing."

"Dad is that your car?"

"Yes dear. Let's get in it and see if we can find some other people that love the Lord."

As they were leaving, someone went to the window. "Hi, how are you all doing?"

"We are looking for some people that love the Lord."

"We do." said James. "This is my wife. Dee, and her mother, Joan. We have two children. Mattie and Jack."

"My name is Roy Green. We have a place that is safe. We will carry you and your daughter. "We do not want for them bad people to find us."

"Thank you. Roy." said James.

"We may have to move on later. We will cross that bridge when we get there. God will help us."

"If you all need anything, we can bring it."

"That is okay. Just bring yourself."

"It is so nice for you all to help us."

"We have seen what is going on out there in this world."

When they got to the place to hide, Roy told the others, "We have some more of God's people. This is James and his daughter, Ruth."

Everyone said. "Hello. Welcome. We all will pray for each other. God loves us, and one day, we will be in heaven."

"We were foolish not to be ready. Pas-tor Jack, would you say a word of prayer so we can get fed?

"My name is Pastor Jack Green. This is my wife, Jeanie We have two sons, Mike and Lewis. I thought we were ready. I did not do what God wanted me to. I was left behind. My wife was doing things she thought were okay. Our two boys we let do what they wanted to do, no love. So we were all left behind."

"We all need to sleep so we can be ready for what may take place."

"Dad, I am scared."

"Honey, everything will be okay."

"Why do some people have lights and some don't?"

"I do not know. We can ask. Maybe someone will answer our question.

"Paul?"

"Yes. Mr. Hall?"

"Why do these people have lights? Did they take the mark?"

"No, they did not. The light people have not made it to their house yet is what I think."

"The TV is on. Look, Dad, the news."

"This is channel 6 News out of Chicago. We have had lots of people calling. They want to know what took our family away from us. Hold on, lady, what can I help you with? My name is Josh Owens out of Chicago."

"I am calling from Alabama. What is going on all over the world? Thousands are none. Where are they?"

"What is your name?"

"Nancy Williams. I went to look for my baby. She is gone."

"Lady, I do not know. I will try to find out."

"Dad, she is crying. Her baby is crone."

"Let's all lie down. Mr. Hall, you can lie down in that room. Your daughter can sleep in the room next to yours."

"Thank you so much. Mrs. Green."

Ruth had a bad night. All she could think of was her mom and Sarah telling her to get ready. She wished she had all her family gone to heaven, except her Dad. like her. was left behind. If anything happened now, she would go to heaven. She is ready. She went to bed. still wishing things could be better.

Some of the others were still up.

"Pastor Jack, do you think we will be okay here?" said Paul.

"I do not know. We can take a walk If you like. We still have lights and water. They may turn it off tomorrow."

"Let's do that." said the pastor. "I have a flashlight in my pocket, and I have the key to get back in. I will tell my wife. Jeanie, we are going for a walk.

"Jeanie. Paul and I are going for a walk."

"You both be safe."

"We will. I just want to see what is going on in town." said the pastor. "We won't be gone long. Jeanie."

When they got to town. Paul said. "Look, Pastor. What is happening? They have so many lined up to be shot. Let's not get too close. They will have us next."

"Let's go back to the house."

It was morning. It was too much. They left and went back home. In the yard, a sheet of paper lay on the around. The pastor picked it up. "I don't think we will need your light."

"I did not know it was so late."

"Paul, it is going to be bad down here."

"I fear for my wife. She is going to have a baby. It is close for it to be born. She has been sick. We think the worse, what they may do to our baby to make us take the mark."

"We will not."

They had a surprise when they got inside-word from the president.

"Warning from the president. This is for the ones that will not take the mark. We will be looking for you. Do not think you will live around us and get what you want. We will not let that happen. The Antichrist will be here with the mark at the Chicago Big House, We will be on the strip, looking for the blue house. There will be some good news for the ones that will take the mark in your head and hand. Be at the meeting. When you come, be ready to listen to the president and the Antichrist. He can help you if you will let him."

"Paul, let's be at that meeting. I want to see what is going on. I need to know what they plan. I know it will be bad for us. I will not take that mark." said the pastor.

"What time to go?"

"Six p.m."

"Pastor, how are we going to live here? They will be looking for us."

"look, someone's pulling up in a car."

"Who is it? Let me see," said the pastor's wife. "Looks like a young girl opened the door. She looks scared."

"My name is Tina. Do any of you all know Elizabeth Moore?"

"I do," said Ruth.

"She was the one that led me to the Lord. I could not make it. Is she here?"

"She was ready for the rapture," said Ruth. "She led my mom on her deathbed to the Lord."

She was a real nice person."

"She sure was." said Ruth. "Why would you think she was still on earth?"

"I did not think that. I was hoping she was because if she were still here, then I knew the rapture had not happened."

"I see. I get your point. I miss her so much."

"I wish I had stayed ready," said Tina.

"I wish I had listened to Sarah, her daughter," said Ruth. "Did you know her, Tina?"

"She did come to church where her mom preached to us. The whole family was there."

"How did you find us?"

"There were some people that picked me up. I guess God led them here."

"God is so good."

"Yes,␣he is," said Tina.

"Are you saved now, Tina?"

"No."

"Let me lead you in a sinner's prayer. You know, Tina, if you do not give your heart to God, it will be easy for you to take the mark."

"Really? I never thought that

"If you don't let God be your leader, then there is no love in your heart. That makes it easier for the devil. You need God now. It is going to get bad.

"Repeat after me, Tina. Dear Jesus, I am a sinner. I ask you to forgive all my sins. I will do your commands. I believe you died on the cross, shed your blood for me. You arose from the grave, and you are with the father. You will come back again to take us home in heaven. I ask this in your sweet name. Amen.

"Now, Tina, you are a born-again Christian. You will go to heaven when Jesus comes for you."

"I do feel different."

"Everyone, this is Tina. Let's all welcome her to the kingdom of God."

"Welcome. Tina." said everyone.

"Pastor, it is close to six p.m. We need to make that meeting."

"Okay, let's go. Jeanie, I will be back in a little. James, do you want to go?"

"Why not. Ruth, I am going with the pastor and Paul to check out what is going on

"Okay, Dad. We will pray for you all."

"Honey, your hair is so pretty."

"Thank you, Dad. It is so long."

"Yes, dear," said her dad.

"You do not worry about your dad. I will be fine. I am sure God has his angels watching over us. We will tell you all what happens."

"Guys, are you both ready?"

"Yes."

"Let's go. We will miss the best part."

When they got to the blue house, everyone were standing outside. Out came the president with a man. They were pushing him.

"Look, Pastor. What is on his head?"

"What"

"Look good. It has God's name on his forehead."

"Wow. They are going to kill him. More coming out."

They were praising God, shouting. As they got outside, angels were with them. I thought they would be inside," said the pastor. Time for the president. Sonic were glad he was there.

"Now we have some good news to tell you. If you take mark, you will be tine. My whole family has the mark. The Antichrist and my family are big buddies. We do not worry anymore. We are all line."

"Mr. President, where do you think the missing people went?"

"Jack, I do not know."

"How can anyone die and come back?"

"Jack, maybe they came from space and got them."

"So you do not believe in the rapture?"

"What are you saving?"

"Mr. President, you are the one leading the USA, and you tell me you believe in spacemen. That is a laugh."

"Do you believe in Jesus?"

"Yes, I do."

"Then, Jack, why are you still here?"

"I was foolish and was left behind."

"Now it is time for the Antichrist. Everyone, let's welcome our new ruler."

"Look, Pastor. Here that devil worshiper comes."

"Hello, hello, let me say I will help you, but you will be under my spell. Let's see what we can do to help you. I know you people saw them ones with God in their heads. They are lost. I will not help them. They have made another way to live." He laughed. "It will be bad for them. We will have peace in our country. Mr. President, is that right?"

"Yes, you said it."

"I am the God you serve. Let me help you. I will be your God. You can come to me anytime you wish."

"Look, Pastor, how them people are around the Antichrist. He has them in his web like the devil has them. He is so mellowed out, like nothing is going to happen."

"Well, it is. Jesus is coming back. He will see. Hell is waiting for them. They will pay. They also will bow to my Jesus and confess he is Lord of lords."

"You are right, Paul. They will get what they are asking for."

"Let's go back to your house, Pastor. It is getting late."

"Look, they are cutting off more of God's people's heads. The ones that have God in their heads. The order is from the president and the Antichrist."

"We better get out of here."

"Wait. Let's see what they are talking about."

"Pastor, we have been here awhile. Maybe we should go home. The family will be worried. We will have to keep off the road. Since all this happened, they will be looking for us."

"Pastor, look at them people. They believe in the Antichrist."

"They do trust him like a god."

"Yes, we will have peace, peace for all you people. I have powers to do what you asked, American people."

"Wow, he does think he is God."

"James, you are quiet."

"I was thinking about my little girl, Ruth. I suppose she is wondering where I am. She just lost her mom last Wednesday, a week ago, to a car wreck. Hit a car, died at the hospital. Those people make me sick."

"Yes," said the pastor. I am going to see if I can talk to some of them people, see if they know Jesus."

He touched the lady in front of him. She looked at the pastor. "Come go with us." She touched her husband and two boys. "You do not want to stand in that line. I am Pastor Green. These are my two friends, James and Paul. You all can go with us."

"We need the flashlight, Pastor."

"As they were walking, the pastor asked, "You folks from around here?"

"This is my husband, Roy, our two boys, Billy and Jack. We are the Jacksons. Yes, we are from here."

"Welcome, Mrs. Jackson. Sorry you missed the rapture."

"Some of us didn't. My little girl, Patty, went in the rapture." It's okay, dear. You will see her again soon."

"She was my baby girl, only two months old. When it happened, I went to look in her crib. She was gone. Her little clothes were all I could see. The TV woke me up, saying something happened to lots of people. I knew what happened. My mom told me about Jesus."

"So did my mom," said her husband.

We knew it would happen. We thought we had plenty of time."

"Are you saved now, Mrs. Jackson?"

"Yes, we are."

"But why were you in the line where the Antichrist was?"

"We saw it in the paper. We wanted to check it out."

"We can talk tomorrow. We need to rest," said the pastor's wife. "There is a bedroom down the hall on the left, Mrs. Jackson. You and your family can sleep there. There are two beds in there. I know all are tired. Let's all find our beds and rest. We will need our strength to pray God will help us."

The next day was Sunday. Everyone went to the kitchen. "We have breakfast ready," said the pastor's wife. "There is some coffee for the ones that drink coffee. We need to get ourselves ready for what's about to happen. Pastor, would you pray over us all?"

"Dear Lord, thank you for our new friends you led us to help. Thank you for the food. In Jesus's name. Amen."

"We can get ready to move in case we have to." Someone pulled up everyone. "Go out the back door." That is what they did.

"I know where we can go," said Paul. "I saw an empty house. Let's all go there. Remember, stay off the highway. They could be looking, for us."

"Who?" said Ruth. "Dad, do we have to keep moving?"

"Yes, we do."

"I am scared."

"We only got God to help us. If they take the mark, all the love leaves their body."

"Dad, is that what happened to people?"

"Yes, dear. They have the devil in them. Anyone that takes it will go to hell, no change. Yes, they can kill you. They do not care. They have no heart."

"Dad, that is so sad."

"Everyone, the house is not empty. We have beds. Let's go to the kitchen, see if there is any food."

"Look, it is full of food," said Ruth. "God must have gotten here before us. We have a place to sleep and food to eat."

"We do not know how long."

"Looks like there are enough beds. Lights are on, water is on, stove works. Everything is nice."

"Yes," said Paul. "God is so good. He will take care of us. We do not have to worry."

"Look," said the pastor. "There is bread to eat."

All at once, they heard a knock on the door.

"Look out the window," said the pastor.

"I will do that," said James. "No car. But there is a man at the door."

"Open the door, James."

"Come on in. Can we help you? It is an angel."

"Yes, God sent me to help you, you all."

"Welcome," said the pastor.

"God's people will be the only ones to see me. God had me to get food for you all, so I come to let you know he is so proud of all of you. Things will happen, but God will help you. There will be some of you that won't face death until you see what is going to happen. It will have to be your family, but God says hold on. Look at what comes after the tribulation, do not look at what is going to happen. Someone is outside. It is the bad men. Go with them. Some of you will die for the Father and be torched. This is for the love of the Lord."

He left. There was a knock. They opened the door.

"You all come with me."

"Where are we going, Dad?"

"Ruth, the angel told us what is going to happen."

"It is time for us to put you all in jail."

That is what they did.

"What is your name, miss?"

"My name is Ruth. My dad is James."

"You come with me."

"No," said Ruth.

"What are you going to do with my daughter?"

"Do you have the mark?"

"Hold on, you guys. Come here. Look at his head. It says God. So does she. They are marked with their God. There is nothing we can do but line them up and kill them."

Jack's wife was going to have a baby. It was at the time she was in jail. All at once it happened. The devil people saw the baby, and they took it. "Will you take the mark?"

"No, I will not."

"Okay, cut the baby's hand off."

"No, please don't do it. She is my baby."

"Lady, we do not care. Are you going to take the mark?"

"No, I will not give up my Lord."

"Okay, kill the baby."

"Oh no, please do not let them kill my baby!"

The Lord spoke to her. "Remember what the angel said? It is happening. You are tested death because your baby will be with me. She will be okay. I will take it before they kill it. Looks bad to you, but God has everything under control."

Just like it was in many things, God took care of the baby before they killed it. She was now in heaven.

"Are you going to take the mark now?"

"No, we will not," said the pastor. "We will not let you take things from us. We love Jesus."

"Billy, come here."

"No, Mom." He was crying. "Take the mark."

"No, we will not."

"Billy, looks like your mom and dad do not care."

"But they do care. I know Mom and Dad care for me. They don't want me to go to hell, and they do not want me to go."

"Billy, Jesus is with you. He will never leave you. Because of what you do for him, he is proud of you."

"Yes, Mom, I will stand up for Jesus."

So they cut off his hands. "Oh no!" The blood was everywhere. "Mom, please help me."

"Honey, pray, ask God to help you."

"It is time for you all to go. I will give you one minute to make up your mind. Are you going to take the mark?"

"No, we will not. We are not going to hell."

"Okay, in jail you will go. You will change your mind when you go without food."

"I am only giving you water and bread. We do not want you to die. See how you like it, preacher, when your family cries because you do not have any food."

"My family will be okay. I do not worry about my family. God will take care of them."

They began to push the preacher and hit him. "Now where is your God?"

"He is here as he said he would be. I do not care what you do."

Back to James and Ruth. . .

"Dad, I wish I had listened to Sarah." know, dear."

"I had time to change."

"I thought I had plenty of time."

"I did too, Dad. Me, so young."

"But age does matter."

"Elizabeth led Mom to Jesus on her deathbed. One day we will all be together."

"Yes, dear."

"Now let's try get to some sleep."

"These beds are so hard."

"But we can count on God to pull us through it."

"Good night, Dad. See you in the morning. Are you awake, Dad?"

"Yes, dear."

"I would like to know the time."

"Here they come with our water and bread they promised us."

"Jesus guys, here is your bread and water."

"I wonder where the rest of our family is."

"I do not know, Dad."

Back to the preacher and his family . . .

"Billy, I am sorry."

In came a man. He put a cloth on Billy's hand. "I love the Lord. God will take care of you. They do not know who I am. They will punish me real bad when they find out."

"My family will pray for you," said Billy.

When the jailer came in, the man pushed the pastor. "That is good. He needs that." Then he walked out.

"Now, preacher, come with me. You and your family, you all must die. You do not want to take the mark."

"No, we will not take it."

As they were getting all the ones ready to shoot, the pastor said, "Dear, I will see my family in heaven." The pastor kissed his wife and told the boys, "Dad loves you. Be brave for Jesus. It will be over fast."

In came the men to take Pastor Green and his family to be killed for Jesus. The boys were crying, "Mom, why did we not get ready? We could have gone in the rapture."

"Kids, your dad and I love you so much."

"Come on, you so-called Christian." Billy was holding on to his dad's hand.

"Bye, Dad. We will meet again in heaven."

"Bye, son, love you."

"We love you and Mom," said the boys. The last words were "See you in heaven."

This is end of my story. People, you need to be ready. Do not be foolish like the pastor and his wife. They also caused the boys to miss the rapture. I know you would not want this to happen. God is the answer. Jesus is coming soon. John 3:16 says, "For God so loved the world that He gave His only son, that whosoever believes in him shall not perish but have everlasting life."

Give God control of your life. He is all you need. This is the end of my story, not my book.

Children are little angels God gave to us. He put them in our hands and hearts to teach his ways and have them learn to understand the ways of our world and about heaven from birth. We do not know how they will react to what we have in store for them, so we teach them one day at a time. Some children are raised in homes with good parents; they know the Bible, how Jesus came to this world to save lost sinners. We have all sinned, have come short of the glory of God. Then there are some that are raised by parents, but not from the Bible. So these children go on doing their thing. They think no one cares. Some of them go to jail for life.

Children are very weak. They need support to make them strong. They can be so lonely inside. They hurt when things go wrong. Kids want to be loved, but they do not know how to show love. That is thanks to their parents for not loving them. They try to tell their parents what is on their minds, but they are left alone to work it out themselves. We are supposed to be the ones to lead our kids through this world because there is no net to catch them when they fall. So they find another way out. Sometimes, it is not good; they can get off the right to the wrong road. God wants our children to live for him.

If one of the parents left home, the children would feel it was their fault. They cannot cope with life. At night when they go to bed, they cry. No one sees their tears; only they can. They feel so alone. The devil can get them in his web. They start running. With children that come from the same household, they will do drugs and other things. The kids will start lying. They will cheat and kill because they have given up all hope in life. Then they are caught between two parents. They will have to make a choice which one to live with.